Jesus and the Gospels
Part II

Professor Luke Timothy Johnson

THE TEACHING COMPANY ®

PUBLISHED BY:

THE TEACHING COMPANY
4151 Lafayette Center Drive, Suite 100
Chantilly, Virginia 20151-1232
1-800-TEACH-12
Fax—703-378-3819
www.teach12.com

ISBN 1-56585-944-8

Luke Timothy Johnson, Ph.D.
Professor of New Testament and Christian Origins, Emory University

Luke Timothy Johnson is the Robert W. Woodruff Professor of New Testament and Christian Origins at the Candler School of Theology, Emory University, in Atlanta, Georgia. Born in 1943 and from the ages of 19 to 28 a Benedictine monk, Dr. Johnson received a B.A. in philosophy from Notre Dame Seminary in New Orleans, an M.Div. in theology from Saint Meinrad School of Theology in Indiana, and an M.A. in religious studies from Indiana University, before earning his Ph.D. in New Testament from Yale University in 1976.

Professor Johnson taught at Yale Divinity School from 1976 to 1982 and at Indiana University from 1982 to 1992 before accepting his current position at Emory. He is the author of 20 books, including *The Writings of the New Testament: An Interpretation* (2nd edition, 1999), which is used widely as a textbook in seminaries and colleges. He has also published several hundred articles and reviews. His most recent publications are: *The Creed: What Christians Believe and Why It Matters* and *The Future of Catholic Biblical Scholarship*. He is working on a study of the influence of Greco-Roman religion on Christianity.

Professor Johnson has taught undergraduates, as well as master's level and doctoral students. At Indiana University, he received the President's Award for Distinguished Teaching, was elected a member of the Faculty Colloquium on Excellence in Teaching, and won the Brown Derby and Student Choice Awards for teaching. At Emory, he has twice received the "On Eagle's Wings Excellence in Teaching" Award. In 1997–1998, he was a Phi Beta Kappa Visiting Scholar, speaking at college campuses across the country.

Professor Johnson is married to Joy Randazzo. They share 7 children, 12 grandchildren, and 3 great-grandchildren. Johnson also teaches the courses called *The Apostle Paul*, *Early Christianity: The Experience of the Divine*, *Practical Philosophy: The Greco-Roman Moralists*, and *Christianity* in Great World Religions for The Teaching Company.

Table of Contents
Jesus and the Gospels
Part II

Jesus and the Gospels

Scope:

Early Christianity was prolific in its production of Gospels—narratives that in one way or another have Jesus of Nazareth as their central character. There are many more Gospels than the four included in the New Testament. They are almost bewilderingly diverse in the way they portray Jesus.

The Gospels are fascinating literary compositions in their own right, and they raise puzzling questions about the figure they portray and about the religious movement, Christianity, that produced them. What accounts for the diversity of images? Is it possible to speak of a single Jesus when accounts about him are so various?

The most common approach to these questions is through history. The so-called "quest for the historical Jesus" asks who the human Jesus really was behind all the different portraits. One example of that quest is offered in the Teaching Company course called *The Historical Jesus*.

Although the historical question is legitimate and even compelling, it is also virtually impossible to answer satisfactorily. Certainly some historical statements can be made about the human Jesus that meet the strictest criteria of historical method. But such statements fall far short of providing a full or even meaningful grasp of Jesus's identity. Worse, such historical efforts treat the actual Gospels shabbily. The literary effect of the compositions tends to be completely ignored, while the materials in them that are deemed authentic are ripped out of their literary contexts to be placed in the historian's reconstruction.

The approach to Jesus and the Gospels taken in this course is not primarily historical but literary. Of course, history comes into play as we place the various Gospels within the development of Christianity. Our search, however, is not for the figure behind the Gospels but for the even more fascinating figure in them. Only after the full range of these literary representations has been considered can the question of "the real Jesus" adequately be posed—and it may not be answerable in strictly historical terms.

Our focus, in short, is not simply on Jesus but also on the Gospels as literary compositions. We want to know how they came to be, how they are related to one another, and how they communicate through their literary structure, plot, character development, themes, and symbolism. It is, after all, as literature that the Gospels influenced history. And it is through literature that present-day readers can continue to encounter Jesus.

The opening lectures set the context for the emergence of the Gospels as distinctive literary expressions: the historical, cultural, and experiential matrix in which Jesus traditions were selected and shaped by early Christian communities. Then, we consider the conditions that required a shift from oral tradition to written composition and the literary relations among the synoptic Gospels.

The four canonical Gospels (those found in the New Testament) of Mark, Matthew, Luke, and John are next examined in considerable detail, precisely as literary expressions that witness to and interpret the Christian community's convictions concerning Jesus. For each Gospel, we consider not only what is being said but also how it is being said. Such attention is appropriate both because of the literary richness of the canonical Gospels and because theirs are the portrayals of Jesus that have exercised the most influence through history.

We turn next to the wide range of apocryphal Gospels (those not found in the New Testament), including the intriguing infancy Gospels of James and Thomas, fragments from lost narrative Gospels deriving from Jewish Christian circles, and finally, the various compositions usually associated with Gnosticism that in one way or another can be considered Gospels.

The final lectures consider the illusive and compelling figure of Jesus, both as he is found in his diverse literary representations and as he is experienced in communities of faith that read the Gospels in the context of worship.

Acknowledgements

Material from *Documents for the Study of the Gospels* edited by David R. Cartlidge and David L. Dungan, is reproduced with permission from Augsburg Fortress, Publishers (Minneapolis, MN).

Material from *The Nag Hammadi Library in English*, 2nd Edition by James M. Robinson, is reproduced with permission from Brill Academic Publishers.

Lecture Thirteen
Gospel of Matthew—Synagogue Down the Street

Scope:

Because Matthew uses Mark's Gospel in constructing his own version of the good news, it is possible to deduce with considerable confidence, from his redaction of Mark as well as material he adds to Mark, his own compositional interests. His portrayal of Jesus as a teacher and as the fulfillment of Torah, together with his interest in instructing the messianic community in the proper understanding of Torah and, finally, his polemic against the leaders of formative Judaism, all point to a context of competition and conversation with Pharisaic Judaism in the period after the Jewish War.

Outline

I. Because Matthew uses Mark's Gospel as one of its main sources, it provides the best example of how redaction criticism can illuminate the setting and purpose of a Gospel.

   A. Matthew's extensive use of Mark suggests a basic approval of Mark's form of the "good news."

      1. Matthew retains the basic plot line from baptism to burial.

      2. In particular, Matthew retains the emphasis on Jesus as the suffering Son of Man (see the passion predictions).

      3. Matthew's passion narrative follows Mark's closely but emphasizes the identity of Jesus as God's Son and the responsibility of the entire Jewish populace for the death of Jesus (27:25).

   B. Although Matthew consistently shortens Mark's diffuse version of stories, requiring a third fewer words to tell the same story (compare Matt 8:28–34 and Mark 5:1–20), he increases the length of the overall narrative with two important additions that also serve to frame the story.

      1. The genealogy and infancy account (chs. 1–2) serve to connect Jesus more firmly with the story of Israel.

2. The explicit resurrection appearances and final commission (28:9–10, 16–20) serve to connect Jesus more closely to the church.

C. Matthew more fundamentally alters the character of Mark's narrative by the addition of substantial discourse material drawn from Q and M; Jesus is not only called teacher, but he teaches extensively by means of long speeches.

II. The structural arrangements that Matthew introduces suggest something about the possible social setting of the Gospel.

A. Matthew interjects two important narrative transitions in 4:17 and 16:21, which provide a broad *narrative* structure: the identity of Jesus the Messiah (1:1–4:16), the preaching of the Messiah (4:17–16:20), and the teaching of the Messiah (16:21–28:20). That these transitions are hard to spot shows that Matthew is less preoccupied than Mark with the story as such.

B. More impressive are the transitions from discourses to narrative (7:28–29; 11:1; 13:53; 19:1; 26:1), which have the effect of creating five great discourses.

1. The discourses are created by the evangelist out of Q and M materials—they are distributed by Luke differently.

2. They are internally organized and topically distributed (thus, the parables in ch. 13 and eschatology in chs. 24–25).

3. The effect of this editing is to create the impression of "five discourses" that roughly correspond to the "five books of Moses."

C. Matthew uses bracketing (*inclusio*) as an organizational principle within discourses and as a means of framing his Gospel as a whole (see 1:23 and 28:20).

D. A consistent (and distinctive) feature of Matthew's Gospel is the frequent use of scriptural citations introduced by set formulas ("this happened in order to fulfill the saying of the prophet").

1. Such interjections represent authorial commentary on the story being told—a "telling" as well as a "showing."
2. The application of Torah to every detail of the Messiah's existence demonstrates the author's concern that Jesus be seen as "according to scripture."

E. The combination of redactional features suggests that the most plausible setting for Matthew's Gospel is one in which "teachers of Torah" are important.

III. Matthew's Gospel is composed in the context of conflict and conversation with formative Judaism in the late 1st century, the "synagogue down the street."

A. *Formative Judaism* designates the Talmudic or Pharisaic tradition as it came into definitive shape after the destruction of the temple (70 C.E.).
1. Based on the religious convictions of the Pharisees and the professional skill of the Scribes, it was the form of Judaism sufficiently adaptable and mobile to survive the catastrophe that was the war with Rome.
2. In the synagogues of the diaspora, the Pharisaic ideals took hold: The observance of Torah was the fulfillment of covenant and the measure of wisdom; the study of Torah was as important as the keeping of the commandments.
3. This formative Judaism was precisely centered in teaching and in Torah.

B. For a community like Matthew's, being expelled from the synagogue for the confession of Jesus as Messiah would have involved a complex process of separation and appropriation.
1. As the reason why they were separated from the synagogue, Jesus would more than ever be the central symbol for the members of the Matthean community.
2. Jesus would also, thereby, gather to himself the symbols that the synagogue down the street used to express its identity.

Essential Reading:

The Gospel of Matthew.

Supplementary Reading:

L. T. Johnson, *The Writings of the New Testament*, pp. 187–211.

J. A. Overmann, *Matthew's Gospel and Formative Judaism: The Social World of the Matthean Community* (Minneapolis: Fortress Press, 1990).

Questions to Consider:

1. What aspects of Matthew's Gospel support the suggestion that it is composed in the context of controversy with the Pharisaic tradition?

2. How does Matthew's addition of narrative material at either end of his Markan source serve to frame and interpret his story?

Lecture Thirteen—Transcript
Gospel of Matthew—Synagogue Down the Street

In the ancient church, Matthew's Gospel was thought to be the first one written. In fact, it was thought to be written by the Matthew who, according to this Gospel, was called from his tax collector's booth. Matthew 9:9 identifies the person whom Mark calls Levi, the son of Alphaeus, as Matthew, the tax collector, and early church writers thought that this was the Matthew who became a follower of Jesus and wrote a Gospel. Matthew's Jewish character, therefore, was thought to be the result of its having been the earliest Gospel written. But in our previous lectures on Mark, we saw that Mark's Gospel was thoroughly Jewish in character. It engaged Jewish apocalyptic literature. Still, Matthew's Gospel is Jewish in a distinctive way, which is why I have called this opening lecture on his Gospel "Matthew: the Synagogue Down the Street."

The solution of the synoptic problem tells us that Matthew used Mark's Gospel in writing his own; that is, there was a copy of Mark's Gospel in writing before him, and Matthew edited Mark as he was composing his own Gospel. This enables us to date Matthew's Gospel approximately around the year 85, which is conventionally done. Why? It is guesswork; it's based on two suppositions. The first is that it takes a little while for Mark's Gospel, which we've dated around the year 70, to move into other areas so it could be used by somebody else. Secondly, it's around this time that scholars have tended to date the 19th benediction, the *Birkat ha minim* used in the synagogues in order to expel messianist Jews from worshiping with non-messianist Jews in the synagogue.

We know that Matthew, sometime a decade and a half after Mark's Gospel was written, sat to write his own Gospel, using Mark as a source. Therefore, Matthew gives us the opportunity for seeing how redaction criticism can eliminate the setting and purposes of a Gospel. What do we mean by redaction criticism? We have already spoken of source criticism, which is exactly what we're doing when we look at Mark as the source for Matthew and Luke, and we've also in this course talked about form criticism, namely, the study of the individual units of the Gospels as they were handed on in oral tradition. By redaction criticism, we mean the way in which Matthew and Luke edited Mark as they were writing their own Gospels.

The first thing that we can observe is that Matthew's extensive use of Mark suggests a basic approval of Mark's form of the good news. Matthew's corrections to Mark are largely by way of diction, grammar, and syntax. He seeks to clarify and provide nuance rather than fundamentally correct what he takes over from Mark. In particular, Matthew retains Mark's emphasis on Jesus as the suffering son of man. Indeed, Matthew even adds a Son of man statement that is not found in Mark's Gospel. In Matthew 8:20, we find Jesus saying that foxes have holes and birds of the air have nests, but the Son of man has nowhere to lay his head. Of particular importance is the fact that Matthew retains Mark's passion predictions, leading up to the passion account of the Gospel, and, when we turn to Matthew's passion account, we see that place in the Gospels in which there is the highest degree of agreement.

For the most part, Matthew follows Mark's passion account fastidiously, with only a few variations. First, Matthew adds material. We call this material that's distinctive to Matthew M material, like the short account of Pilate's wife sending him a message during Jesus's trial before Pilate, or the account of the death of Judas, or the account of the dead rising from their tombs in the city of Jerusalem at the death of Jesus, or the story about the placing of soldiers at the tomb to prevent Jesus's disciples from robbing it. These are simple Matthian additions to Mark's passion account.

He also adds a slight nuance to the identity of Jesus as God's son. We saw in Mark's Gospel that his executioner, the centurion, cries out, "This was truly God's son" on seeing Jesus's death. In Matthew's Gospel, the crowds of people that pass by mocking Jesus mock him in terms of, "If you are God's son, come down from the cross," an aspect which is missing in Mark, so a slight greater emphasis on Jesus's identity as God's son. We'll pick up this theme later. More troubling, a greater emphasis on the responsibility of the entire Jewish populace for the death of Jesus. It is Matthew's Gospel alone that has the notorious cry of the people, "His blood be upon us and upon our children." The so-called blood curse that was so responsible for the long history of Christian anti-Semitism on the charge of deicide is found in Matthew's Gospel; this is found in Matthew 27:25, I hope that these presentations will help contextualize that particular statement.

When we look at the rest of Matthew's Gospel, we see that Matthew consistently shortens Mark's diffused version of individual stories. We said that Mark was very wordy, very pleonastic. Often, Matthew requires about a third fewer words to tell the same story. An example is the story of the Gergesene demoniac. In our lecture on Mark, we saw that this is a very long story, Mark 5:1-20, and gets into very significant detail about the man who had the demons driven out of him, what happened to him before, what happened to him after. Notice Matthew's version:

28: When he came to the other side, to the country of the Gergesenes, two demoniacs met him, (not one, but two) coming out of the tombs, so fierce that no one could pass that way.

29: And behold, they cried out, "What have you to do with us, O Son of God? Have you come here to torment us before the time?"

30: Now a herd of many swine was feeding at some distance from them.

31: And the demons (plural) begged him, "If you cast us out, send us away into the herd of swine."

32: He said to them, "Go." So they came out and went into the swine; and behold, the whole herd rushed down the steep bank into the sea, and perished in the waters.

33: The herdsmen fled, going into the city they told everything, and what had happened to the demoniac.

34: And behold, all the city came out to meet Jesus; and when they saw him, they begged him to leave their neighborhood.

What happened to this guy? What Matthew has done is tremendously shortened the story, tidied it up, and he has dealt with the fact that the demon spoke in the plural in Mark's Gospel by making two demoniacs and thus tidying up the language. This is a good example of Matthew's way of editing Mark. So if we had only Matthew's editing of Mark, it would be a shorter Gospel rather than an enormously longer Gospel. But Matthew adds material. First, he adds two significant narrative pieces. In the beginning of the Gospel, before the baptism of John the Baptist, Matthew adds a genealogy of Jesus and an infancy account in Chapters 1-2, which serve to connect Jesus more firmly within the story of Israel. We'll look at that in our next lecture.

At the end of the story, Matthew adds an explicit resurrection appearance. The women don't leave the empty tomb in fear and tell no one; they go off and they encounter the risen Jesus, and then they tell the disciples, and then Matthew adds a further appearance of Jesus up on the mountain. At that final appearance of Jesus to the Eleven after his resurrection, Matthew has Jesus give them a great commission, which concludes his Gospel. "All authority in heaven and on earth has been given to me. Go therefore and make disciples of all nations, baptizing them in the name of the Father and of the Son and of the Holy Spirit, teaching them to observe all that I have commanded you; and lo, I am with you always, to the close of the age."

Matthew has added to the narrative by a prologue and an epilogue, if you will, one connecting Jesus more explicitly to Israel, the other connecting Jesus more explicitly to the life of the church. But Matthew more fundamentally alters the character of Mark by adding enormous amounts of sayings material drawn from the hypothetical source Q and his own particular source M. In Matthew's Gospel, Jesus is not only called teacher, he teaches all the time, and teaches extensively and by means of long speeches. Matthew's Gospel is not only 28 chapters, compared to Mark's 16 chapters; it's actually much longer because of the way in which he has reduced the narrative length of Mark and added in all this additional discourse material.

Let's look now at the structural arrangements that Matthew uses in shaping his story. I want to remind you again, in the Greek manuscripts there are no chapter divisions, there are no verse divisions, there are no helpful editorial paragraph headings that say, "Here's where the Sermon on the Mount begins." There's nothing of that and so we have to rely upon the signals that the author himself gives us. We will see that the way that Matthew has arranged his material also points to the possible social setting of this Gospel. Let's look first at two important narrative transitions that Matthew provides in Chapter 4, Verse 17, and Chapter 16, Verse 21. In Chapter 4, Verse 17, Matthew notes from this time on Jesus began to preach the kingdom of heaven, and then in 16:21 from this time on, Jesus began to teach his disciples. Those narrative transitions provide a kind of broad narrative structure.

The first section of Matthew from 1:1 to 4:16 is the identity of Jesus the Messiah, established by the genealogy, his birth, his baptism, and his testing in the wilderness. From 4:17 to 16:20, the preaching of the Messiah, and from 16:21 to 28:20 the teaching of the Messiah. It must be said that these transitions are so hard to spot, and seem to affect our reading of the story so little, that it is an indication that Matthew is much less preoccupied than Mark is with narrative as such, as with story as such. Much more impressive are the transitions that Matthew establishes. From discourse to narrative in the outline. I have indicated five of these transitions, 7:28-29, 11:1, 13:53, 19:1 and 26:1, and the effect of them is to create five great discourses.

Let me read simply the first of these transitions in 7:28-29, "And when Jesus finished these sayings, the crowds were astonished at his teaching, for he taught them as one who had authority, and not as their scribes." Matthew does not provide these at the beginning of the discourse, but at the end, as he shifts from discourse to further narrative. When he came down from the mountain, the story then continues. What is the effect of these? The effect is that we have long discourses; Jesus is speaking continuously.

What is very important to note is that the discourses in Matthew's Gospel are the invention and the creation of Matthew. It is Matthew's Sermon on the Mount, not Jesus'. It is Matthew's discourse on the church, not Jesus'. Matthew has drawn from the Q material, those sayings materials and possibly the oral tradition, and has woven them together into the form of these discourses. Notice that the same Q materials are distributed by Luke quite differently. Whereas Matthew has a Sermon on the Mount, which extends from Chapter 5-7, three full chapters, Luke has Jesus delivering a sermon on the plain, not on the mountain, which is less than a full chapter. And many of the sayings that Matthew has in the Sermon on the Mount, Luke puts into Jesus's long final journey to Jerusalem in Luke, Chapters 9-19. This indicates that Matthew has constructed the discourses.

Secondly, these discourses are internally organized. Matthew uses a variety of rhetorical techniques to give them internal coherence, thus, in the sermon on the mount, the beatitudes, the antitheses, the statements on prayer, fasting, and alms giving, and then further statements and a nice conclusion about the one who builds his house upon sand and the one who builds his house upon rock. And it's similar with the other discourses, so they are internally organized, and they are topically distributed. So the first discourse, which is conventionally called the Sermon on the Mount, we have the conditions of discipleship and life within the kingdom; in Chapter 10, the conditions of the mission on which Jesus sends the Twelve; in Chapter 13, the parables; in Chapter 18, the eternal life of the community; and in Chapters 24 through 25, we have the eschatological discourse much expanded from Mark.

Again, these are like the Teaching Company's lectures on various topics. The five great discourses of Jesus are distributed throughout Matthew's Gospel, and so the effect of this editing is to create the impression of five discourses that even in the early church were recognized as roughly equivalent to the five books of Moses, and so we have this sense of Jesus being portrayed as the new Moses, who is, in effect, delivering a new law, if you will, a new Torah, through these five great discourses. This may be a little too neat because it doesn't fall out quite that neatly, but we can't help but get some kind of impression of Jesus as the new Moses when the first of these discourses begins in Chapter 5, Verses 1-2: "Seeing the crowds, he went up on the mountain, and when he sat down his disciples came to him. And he opened his mouth and taught them, saying: 'Blessed are the poor in spirit.'" Clearly Jesus's going up on the mountain, sitting, discoursing, is a Matthian creation to give the impression of a new Moses.

Finally, I should just observe about these discourses is that's why Matthew is so difficult to read, basically. It's sort of like a typical student's day in class: You get up, you go to class and sit down and listen to somebody for an hour, and then you walk to lunch, and then you go to another class. In a day that's interspersed by sermons, you don't get much of a sense of a dramatic flow of plot, so in Mark, we're caught up in the drama of discipleship because Mark moves us along that way. In Matthew, we have to sit down—if you have a red-letter edition of the Bible you can see these great blocks of material—we have to sit down once in a while and listen to a long lecture, and that makes all the difference. Matthew is much less about the story and much more about what Jesus says.

A final technique that Matthew uses in organizing this material is called bracketing, or *inclusio*. You'll remember that when I spoke about Mark, I talked about Mark's way of putting one story within the other, kind of a sandwiching technique, so that we were forced to look at these together. Matthew uses that same kind of bracketing technique, but he tends to use it with larger chunks of material, not A-B-C closely locked together, but rather larger bodies of material which face each other, and the most impressive of these is the *inclusio* that brackets his Gospel as a whole. Notice in Chapter 1, Verse 23, when the birth of Jesus is announced, "His name shall be called Emmanuel," and then Matthew interjects "which means God with us," and the Gospel of Matthew concludes with the statement, "Behold, I am with you alway," so God is with us in Jesus's birth; Jesus is with us through the resurrection and the teachings of Jesus. So Matthew brackets his entire narrative in this fashion.

A final, important, consistent, and distinctive feature of Matthew's Gospel is the frequent use of scriptural citations. I mentioned on Mark that Mark does not actually quote scripture often. He uses scripture a lot, but he doesn't quote it often; when he does, he does it very purposefully. Matthew quotes scripture all the time, giving full citations of scripture, and he does so in a very characteristic way. He introduces them by means of a set formula. This happened in order to fulfill the saying of the prophet, or this happened in order to fulfill the scripture that says.

What do we have here with this? Such interjections represent authorial commentary on the story being told. Remember we saw how Mark looks out at the reader and said "let the reader understand," indicating that Mark is well aware that he's not only telling a story about the past but he's telling a story about the past to readers. Matthew does the same thing. It is an example of what Wayne Booth would call in his classic book, *The Rhetoric of Fiction,* telling and not just showing. Matthew interrupts the story, looks out at the reader and says, "This particular thing that I've just told you happened in order to fulfill a scripture passage from the past." It is an authorial commentary on his own story, and the effect is that Matthew applies Torah to every detail of the Messiah's existence. We see these formula citations from the very first part of Matthew's infancy account all the way to the passion account, and it shows the author's concern that Jesus throughout his ministry be seen as according to scripture.

In sum then, the combination of redactional features, editing features that I have identified, the addition of discourses, the setting off of these discourses, clearly shows Jesus as teacher, and, thirdly, these formula citations from Torah suggests that the most plausible setting for Matthew's Gospel is one in which teachers, and specifically teachers of Torah, are important. It is from these clues that we begin to move to a suggestion concerning the social setting of Matthew's Gospel and its historical setting. I propose, along with a pretty well established body of contemporary scholarship, that Matthew's Gospel is composed in the context of conflict and conversation with formative Judaism in the late first century, what I am calling here "the synagogue down the street."

My conceit of "the synagogue down the street" actually has an archaeological basis. Yale archaeologists in the 1930s uncovered the city of Doura Europos, which is a Roman city on the Euphrates in Iraq, which was on the very border of the Parthian Empire, and it was destroyed by an invasion of the Parthians in the year 250 of the Common Era. But archaeologists discovered as they dug up that city that on Wall Street, which was the street facing the Euphrates, almost side by side, down the same street was a Mithraeum, a meeting place for the god Mithras, a Jewish synagogue, and a Christian house church, so that there was this sort of social context in which people would be aware of what was going on in each other's building, and in fact the artwork in each of those buildings was dramatically similar.

Formative Judaism designates what we sometimes call Talmudic Judaism or classical Judaism or rabbinic Judaism. What do we mean? We mean the Pharisaic tradition as it came to definitive shape after the destruction of the temple. Remember, before the temple was destroyed in the year 70, there were a variety of sects within Judaism: the Sadducees, who were mostly aligned with the aristocracy and the high priestly family and for whom the temple was the main symbol of Jewish identity; the Zealots, who were military resisters and whose main symbol for Judaism was the kingship, or the kingdom; the Essenes, who withdrew from other Jews and for whom the central symbol was the land and the purification of the land; and, finally, the Pharisees, for whom the central symbol for Jews were the texts of Torah itself.

After the year 70, these other groups fell away. No more temple, no more Sadducees; the Zealots are whipped by the Romans. The Essenes, who joined the Zealots at the end, were also destroyed by the Romans, so the Pharisees had a form of Judaism which was flexible and survivable, and so it became the dominant form of Judaism after the fall of the temple and entered into a sibling rivalry with this new group of people who calls themselves Jews, namely, the followers of Jesus. This form of Judaism is based on the religious convictions of the Pharisees and the professional skill of those called scribes, *sophorim*, book people. It was a form of Judaism that was sufficiently adaptable and mobile to survive the catastrophe that was the war with Rome.

Notice the Sadducees had as their symbol a building; the Zealots, a kingship; the Essenes, the land. Once those are destroyed, the only two groups that survive as sibling rivals are those who have highly mobile symbols. Torah is a mobile symbol and a resurrected messiah is an extraordinarily mobile symbol. What happens is that in the synagogues of the Diaspora the Pharisaic ideals took hold so that Judaism, as it moved out of Palestine, became Pharisaic Judaism in the Diaspora as well. The observance of Torah was the fulfillment of covenant and the measure of wisdom. The study of Torah was as important as the keeping of the commandments, and this formative Judaism was precisely centered in the relationship between rabbis and disciples in the use of Midrash and in the study of Torah.

For a community like Matthew's, which was expelled from "the great synagogue down the street," remember, it's important to note that in this period we are in a power relationship which is just the opposite of what happens later when Christianity became the imperial religion. In this period, Judaism is far more populous, far more ancient, far more wealthy, far more powerful than this tiny little sect, so what happens when a community is expelled from the great synagogue down the street and has to occupy the store front assembly down the road in a shabby part of town? Precisely for the confession of Jesus as Messiah, this community would be caught up in a complex process of separation and appropriation of symbols.

Jesus is the reason why they're kicked out of the synagogue, so Jesus would become the focus of separation. He would more than ever be the central symbol for the Matthian community. But he would also thereby gather to himself the symbols that "the synagogue down the street" used to express its own identity, so, in other words, Jesus is going to attract to himself all of the symbols that that tradition connected to Torah. You take the symbols of a larger tradition and attach them to your central figure. Matthew's Gospel then is one that is best read as a reflection on Jesus for a church in conflict and conversation with formative Judaism in the last portion of the 1st century.

Lecture Fourteen
Gospel of Matthew—The Messiah of Israel

Scope:

Matthew is concerned to show that Jesus is truly the Messiah of Israel, the one spoken of by the prophets. One manifestation of this concern is the genealogy with which his Gospel opens and his infancy account—a feature shared with Luke's Gospel but with no shared narrative elements—which locate Jesus within the story of Israel. Also illustrative of this concern is his use of explicit scriptural citations (often introduced by set formulas) that serve to prove that Jesus fulfills the prophecies, from his birth to his death.

Outline

I. The opening of Matthew's Gospel establishes Jesus's identity as Son of David and Son of God (chs. 1–2).

   A. The genealogy imitates a literary feature of Torah (the *toledoth*) and connects Jesus to the family of Abraham.
      1. Matthew's genealogy is different from Luke's in structure, placement, and emphasis.
      2. Jesus is descended from Abraham and is the Son of David.
      3. Matthew's inclusion of women in the genealogy points to the role of Mary: Each woman (Tamar, Rahab, Ruth, and the wife of Uriah Bathsheba) represents a certain degree of foreignness and has something sexually suspect in her history; this hints at the sexual ambiguity of the birth of Jesus through Mary.

   B. In Matthew's infancy account, Joseph, rather than Mary, is the main figure.
      1. It is noteworthy that the standard Christmas story represents an amalgam of the infancy accounts of Matthew and Luke, which are very different from each other.

2. Matthew's use of formula citations places all the events under the umbrella of Torah (1:23, 2:6, 2:15, 2:18, 2:22). For example, Matthew recalls that the prophet Micah (Matthew 2:6) prophesized that the Messiah would be born in Bethlehem. Matthew's applications of these prophetic texts are made ex post factum.

3. Of particular significance is the citation from Hosea 11:1 (2:15), which identifies Jesus as "Son of God" within the tradition of Torah. Although there are nuances of divinity in Matthew's portrayal of Jesus (as there are in Mark's), Matthew's reference to Jesus as God's Son here is most likely to be a personification of Israel. Israel was taken out of Egypt and called "my son." Thus, Jesus, as a representative of the best of what God looked for in Israel the obedient one comes to be called "Son of God."

II. The beginning of Jesus's ministry shows Jesus to have a unique relationship to God and, therefore, a unique authority to teach.

A. Matthew expands the role given to John the Baptist who, like Jesus, proclaims "the kingdom of heaven."

1. A consistent emphasis in Matthew is that to be an authentic child of Abraham, you must do the works of repentance.

2. John preaches to the people and threatens them with eschatological judgment (3:4–12).

3. Jesus's baptism by John is a fulfillment of "all righteousness" (3:15).

4. Jesus later explicitly identifies John the Baptist as the expected Elijah (17:9–11).

B. Matthew opens up the baptism scene, making it a public proclamation by God that Jesus is God's beloved Son (3:16–17).

C. Matthew uses Q material to expand the account of Jesus's sojourn in the desert.

1. Jesus experiences three testings presented to him as "Son of God" to be a Messiah according to ordinary human expectations.
2. Matthew shows Jesus as radically obedient to God's words as expressed in Torah and, therefore, capable of interpreting Torah.

D. An aspect of Matthew's hostility to Jewish rivals is the way he has the taunts from the crowd at the crucifixion of Jesus echo the temptations presented Jesus by the devil (27:40, 43).

III. Matthew follows Mark's account of Jesus's ministry fairly closely but with some interesting twists.

A. Matthew is fond of doublets, keeping Mark's (see the double feeding of the multitude) and adding some of his own: Jesus heals two Gerasene demoniacs (9:28–34) and two blind men—twice! (9:27–31; 20:29–34).

B. Matthew uses the formula citations to show that every aspect of Jesus's life and ministry is in fulfillment of Torah.
1. Jesus's preaching fulfills the prophecy of Isaiah 8:23 (4:14).
2. Jesus's acts of healing point to him as the fulfillment of the suffering servant predicted by Isaiah 53:4 (8:17) and Isaiah 42:1–4 (12:15-21).
3. Jesus's teaching in parables fulfills the prophecy of Isaiah 6:9–10 (13:14–15) and Psalm 78:2 (13:34–35).
4. Jesus's royal entry into Jerusalem fulfills (literally) the prophecies of Isaiah 62:11 and Zechariah 9:9 (21:5).
5. Even Jesus's betrayal by Judas is in fulfillment of a (combined) prophecy from Jeremiah 18:2–3; 32:6–9 and Zechariah 11:12–13 (27:9–10).

Essential Reading:
The Gospel of Matthew, 1–4.

Supplementary Reading:
R. E. Brown, *The Birth of the Messiah*, enlarged ed. (New York: Doubleday, 1993).

D. C. Allison, *The New Moses: A Matthean Typology* (NovTSupp 18; Leiden: Brill, 1993).

Questions to Consider:

1. What is the effect of Matthew's shaping of the baptism and temptation account on his portrait of Jesus?

2. How do the "formula citations" represent Matthew's authorial commentary on his own narrative?

Lecture Fourteen—Transcript
Gospel of Matthew—The Messiah of Israel

Matthew's redaction of his Markan source and his addition of sayings materials in the form of five great discourses and his concern to show that Jesus fulfils Torah by his use of formula citations, all these features I have suggested point to a context in which Matthew is engaging formative Judaism in "the synagogue down the street" in the last part of the f^t century. Matthew is not more Jewish than Mark, it is simply differently Jewish, and it is obviously Jewish to us because it engages that form of Judaism with which we are familiar, the form of Judaism that became classical over a period of 2,000 years and is still recognizable in our world today. Nevertheless, as I will show in this lecture, Matthew is, within that context, very much concerned to show that Jesus is Messiah not simply in virtue of his resurrection but very much also the Messiah of Israel.

He begins at once with the opening of his Gospel by establishing Jesus's identity as son of David and son of God. You will remember how abruptly Mark's Gospel opens. Mark simply gives us the title and then John the Baptist, nothing about where Jesus came from or his childhood. Matthew gives us two full chapters on that. The genealogy introduces his Gospel in Chapter 1, Verses 1-17, and that very feature shows his immersion in the world of Torah because the *toledoth,* or genealogy, is consistently used in the Old Testament to introduce major characters. In the first 11 chapters of Genesis, every character is introduced by means of such a toledoth, a genealogy, so much so that the letter to the Hebrews remarks over the extraordinary fact that Melchizedek is not introduced with the genealogy, which for the author of Hebrews can only be understood by the fact that Melchizedek had no mother or father, so there was a very consistent feature, and what it does is connect Jesus to the family of Abraham, which means it connects Jesus to Judaism.

Let's remind ourselves of the wrong question to ask here. The wrong question to ask is, "Does this give an accurate account of Jesus's genealogy?" That's the historical question which we could not possibly answer, most of all because Luke gives us quite a different genealogy. We have two genealogies of Jesus which are quite different. But just common sense would indicate to us that Matthew would scarcely have access to the city files in Jerusalem or that a figure as obscure as Jesus would have his genealogy recorded. No, what we have here is a literary invention, and we have a literary construction that's based for the most part upon the simple Biblical record, and where names are lacking in the Biblical record, they are supplied from some other source, and there may be some traditions involved, but we can't determine that.

In any case, it's obvious that Matthew's genealogy was one that was constructed without consultation with Luke, and this is one of the reasons why I said in an earlier lecture, to me it is so implausible that Luke used Matthew to write his Gospel because it's not at all obvious how Luke could have had Matthew's genealogy in front of him and ended up with the one that he does have. Notice that Luke places his genealogy in a very different place. Luke puts Jesus's genealogy immediately after the baptism of Jesus. Matthew puts it at the very front of the Gospel. Luke's genealogy works backwards; it begins with the statement that Jesus was thought to be the son of Joseph and then son of, son of, son of, moving all the way back not to Abraham but to Adam and son of God, so it moves in a different order. It has different names: it's placed differently in the Gospel.

It is Matthew, therefore, who has constructed the form of this genealogy. Notice the careful noting of generations, seven generations, 14 generations, 14 generations, 14 generations. These multiples of seven extending from Abraham to David, David to Jesus, are clearly a device to indicate the fullness of time represented by the birth of Jesus. Matthew shows us that Jesus is descended from Abraham and therefore he is Jewish.

Secondly, he is descended from David, so that David is the pivotal figure in the genealogy, and therefore Jesus belongs to the Davidic line of kingship within Israel. An interesting feature of Matthew's genealogy, which otherwise is entirely through the male line, is the inclusion of four women in the genealogy: Tamar, Rahab, Ruth, and then (not by name but by reference) the wife of Uriah, who was slain by David, whom we know as Bathsheba. The presence of these four names is perhaps best explicated on the basis that each of these women represent both a certain degree of foreignness to the people and thus the notion that the people can be enriched from outside, but also every one of these characters has something sexually suspect connected to them, and therefore the genealogy of Jesus in the distaff side points to the figure of the sexual ambiguity of the birth of Jesus in the Virgin Mary.

When we go beyond the genealogy to Matthew's infancy account, one of the striking features we notice is that it is not Mary who is the hero but, rather, Joseph. In Luke's version, Mary is the one who receives messages from God; Mary is the one who believes and interprets events. In Matthew's account, Mary is almost completely passive; it is Joseph who is the obedient one. And we should mention here again—you know this, I'm sure, but you do understand that the standard Christmas story represents an amalgam of the infancy accounts of Matthew and Luke. In fact, the two infancy accounts have nothing in common except the names of Jesus's parents and of Jesus himself. They tell completely different stories. So Matthew has the Magi; Luke has the shepherds. Luke has Mary as the hero; Matthew has chosen Joseph as the hero.

But Joseph emerges as a striking figure. Notice when he discovers in Chapter 1, Verse 19, that Mary is pregnant by the Holy Spirit, Matthew says, "Her husband Joseph, being a just man and unwilling to put her to shame, resolved to divorce her quietly. But as he was considering this, an angel of the Lord appeared to him in a dream, saying, 'Joseph, son of David—so again Jesus's Davidic lineage is established through Joseph—do not fear to take Mary your wife, for that which is conceived in her is of the Holy Spirit; she will bear a son and you will name him Jesus, for he will save his people from their sins,'" so the Jewish Hebrew name Yehoshua, Joshua, means "Yahweh saves," the Lord saves, so the name Jesus is a name that refers to the salvation of the people.

Again, then we note that "Joseph woke from sleep and did as the angel of the Lord commanded him; he took his wife, but knew her not until she had borne a son." Again in Chapter 2, Verse 13, Joseph has another dream to bring the child and escape from Herod's wrath to Egypt, and he does so. Again, in 2:19, Joseph receives a vision in a dream by an angel of the Lord, "Now take this child, take the child home," and finally in Chapter 2, Verse 22, we see Joseph for a final time warned in a dream, and he withdraws to the region of Galilee, so Joseph is very much the son of David, who protects Jesus and makes sure that he is preserved as the Messiah.

The other feature we notice in the infancy account in Matthew is that all of the things that happen in the birth and infancy of Jesus are covered by Torah. Here we begin to see Matthew's use of formula citations. Notice the first, in Chapter 1, Verse 23, all this took place to fulfill what the Lord had spoken by the prophet, "Behold, a virgin shall conceive and bear a son, and his name shall be called Emmanuel." Again in Chapter 2, Verse 6, the fact that Jesus was born in Bethlehem is covered by the prophet Micah, Chapter 5, Verse 2, "And you, O Bethlehem, in the land of Judah, are by no means least among the rulers of Judah; for from you shall come a ruler who will govern my people." Again in Chapter 2, Verse 15, when Jesus is taken out of Egypt, Matthew notes, "This was to fulfill what the Lord had spoken by the prophet, 'Out of Egypt I have called my son.'"

In Chapter 2:18, when Herod slaughters the children, the innocents, Matthew quotes Jeremiah, Chapter 40, Verse 1, "This fulfilled what was spoken by the prophet Jeremiah: 'A voice was heard in Ramah, wailing and loud lamentation, Rachel weeping for her children; she refused to be consoled, because they were no more.'" And finally in Chapter 2, Verse 22, when Joseph brings Jesus to Nazareth, Matthew notes, "that what was spoken by the prophets might be fulfilled, 'He shall be called a Nazarene.'" This is very difficult because there is no such scriptural passage; Matthew seems to be making a broad allusion, possibly to Isaiah, Chapter 11, Verse 1, where the Hebrew word *nazer*, branch, is connected to the messiah, but, in any case, we recognize that all of these applications of prophetic text to the birth of Jesus are ex post facto. They are found in Torah because Jesus is from Nazareth. Jesus didn't go to Nazareth because the prophets said he will be called a Nazarene.

I do want to indicate the particular significance of the citation from Hosea 11:1 in Chapter 2,Verse 15, which identifies Jesus as son of God within the tradition of Torah. "Out of Egypt, I have called my son." Christian readers in particular have a tendency of reading anachronistically because they read from the perspective of 2,000 years of Christian belief, so when they see the title son of God in one of the Gospels, they automatically conclude that the Gospel writer is speaking Christian doctrine, and that Jesus is being identified ontologically as participating in the divine nature. One can argue that such creedal developments are perfectly legitimate, and that is the implication of the entire story of Jesus. But one must also be very careful to note that this is not likely what Matthew meant by calling Jesus God's son, number one, because Matthew is not a Greek philosopher and is not thinking ontologically, so the whole notion of a metaphysical characterization of Jesus is simply not in the cards.

Rather, the notion of being God's son means within Judaism the idea of being a specially elect person, one who is in a special relationship with God, but it is a way of being human, and although there are nuances of divinity in Matthew's portrayal of Jesus, just as in Mark's, we have to be careful to recognize that here what we have is a personification of Israel. Israel was taken out of Egypt and called my son, "out of Egypt I am called my son," so for Matthew, Jesus, son of Abraham, son of David, is son of God because he personifies the best of what God looked for in Israel, so it is because Jesus is the obedient one that he is called God's son, and the fate of Jesus therefore and the fate of the people in Matthew's Gospel are very much caught up together.

If we look now at the beginning of Jesus's ministry in Matthew's Gospel, we saw that the beginning of Mark's Gospel was particularly important in terms of setting the table, and it would be helpful for us now to compare Matthew's beginning of the ministry to Mark to show again the distinctive Matthian traits that are revealed. The beginning of Jesus's ministry shows Jesus to have a unique relationship to God and therefore a unique authority to teach. If we look at Chapter 3, we notice first that Matthew expands the role given to John the Baptist. We see first that Matthew has John proclaim the very same thing that Jesus proclaims, "Repent, for the kingdom of heaven is at hand."

But Matthew corrects Mark by giving the full citation from the prophet Isaiah, "the voice of one crying in the wilderness, prepare the way of the Lord; make his path straight." You'll recall that Mark had "as the prophet Isaiah said," but then gave a mixed citation from Malachi and Isaiah. Matthew corrects this scriptural citation, so it is entirely from the prophet Isaiah, and then he follows Mark in describing the clothing and the diet of John the Baptist in 3:4-6, but we pick up in 3:7, and we see that Matthew here attributes to John a prophetic ministry in which he actually challenges the people. When John saw many of the Pharisees coming for baptism, he begins to challenge them, calling them a brood of vipers, that they need to do the works that befit repentance.

Notice, "Do not presume to say to yourselves, 'We have Abraham as our father,' for I tell you, God is able from these stones to raise up children to Abraham. Even now the axe is laid to the root of the trees; every tree therefore that does not bear good fruit is cut down and thrown into the fire." What we see here in the mouth of John the Baptist is the sense that to be an authentic child of Abraham is not simply a matter of birth, and that there is going to be a division within the people, that you have to do the works of repentance, the works that are befitting of the children of Abraham, in order to be a real member of the Jewish people, and for Matthew's Gospel this is going to be a consistent sort of emphasis. We see that Matthew has John threatening the people with judgment in Verses 7-12 of Chapter 3.

When Matthew brings Jesus to the moment of baptism, we have this puzzling exchange. I'm reading from 3:13-17: "Then Jesus came from Galilee to the Jordan to John, to be baptized by him. John would have prevented him, saying, 'I need to be baptized by you, and do you come to me?'" What we find here is a reflection of the perception in antiquity that the greater person baptizes the lesser person, and, furthermore, that John's baptism was a baptism of repentance from sin. Mark apparently wasn't aware of the problem and didn't deal with it. John just baptized Jesus, but Matthew is clearly aware of the implications here of should Jesus be considered as inferior to John and was Jesus in need of a baptism of repentance from sin, so we have this little Gaston-Alfonse routine between Jesus and John the Baptist.

John says, "No, I need to be baptized by you, and do you come to me?" but Jesus says "Let it be so now, for thus it is fitting for us to fulfill all righteousness and then he consents." In other words, Jesus is deferring to John and Jesus's baptism is an act of righteousness, not a cleansing from sin. Notice in the baptism of Jesus by John we have the announcement from heaven is in Matthew's version a public announcement. In Mark, only Jesus and the readers knew that God had designated him as the beloved son. Here in Matthew, the voice from heaven says "This is my beloved son with whom I am well pleased," so it is a designation of Jesus as a publicly identified messiah for the people. Later, Matthew has Jesus explicitly identify John the Baptist as that expected Elijah, the one that Malachi had said God would send before his chosen one to prepare the people, so in every respect Jesus is an authorized Jewish messiah within Matthew's Gospel.

Immediately after the baptism of Jesus—notice that he was called God's son when he was taken out of Egypt; now he's designated as God's son in the baptism. So we turn to Chapter 4, Verses 1-11, and the temptation account. In Mark, what did we find? In Mark, we found that the spirit threw Jesus out into the wilderness, he was tempted by the devil, he was with the wild beasts, and he was ministered to by the angels. We found it one of the most puzzling passages in Mark's Gospel; we didn't know quite what was being said. Matthew takes that tiny Markan passage and expands it by the addition of Q material. We call it Q material because it's also in Luke's Gospel at this point. This is material that both Matthew and Luke share but Mark does not have.

Now, Jesus is led up by the spirit into the wilderness precisely in order to be tested by the devil. In other words, both Matthew and Luke have constructed this as a sort of messianic testing of Jesus. Are you morally worthy of being the Messiah? You've been anointed; now do you have the stuff? So we have the threefold testing of Jesus by the devil. Two interesting features—notice the function of quoting the scripture. This is where we get the line that the devil can quote scripture to his own ends, so it's Jesus who quotes scripture. It's in the next one that the devil quotes scripture. In the first one, we have the tempter come and say to him, "If you are the son of God, command these stones to become loaves of bread," and Jesus answers, "It is written, `Man shall not live by bread alone, but by every word that proceeds from the mouth of God.'"

Again, "If you are the son of God, throw yourself down," and now the devil quotes scripture: "He will give his angels charge of you." Jesus answers the scripture, and finally a third testing, "I will give you all these kingdoms if you fall down and worship me," and Jesus quotes scripture "You shall worship the Lord, your God, and him only shall you serve." So we have here, notice, this testing of Jesus precisely as God's son. What is Matthew showing us? Matthew is showing us two things. First, Jesus is radically obedient to God according to the norms of Torah itself. He is therefore worthy of teaching Torah. Jesus is completely obedient to Torah, and therefore he is authorized to teach others how to understand Torah.

Also, Matthew has cleverly constructed this entire sequence to help us see Jesus as the personification of Israel and of Moses. Notice "out of Egypt I called my son" in the infancy account. He passes through the waters of baptism and is called, "You are my beloved son." He passes through the wilderness and is tested, but unlike the people of Israel, who tested God and who rebelled and did not obey, Jesus is perfectly obedient, so he then comes out of the desert and then in Chapter 5, Verse 1, he goes up on the mountain, sees his disciples, opens his mouth and teaches them, so if Jesus in Chapter 5, Verses 1-2, appears as Moses giving the Decalogue, Matthew has prepared for that by calling him out of Egypt, calling him son, showing him in the wilderness and tested by God and worthy to be an interpreter of Torah.

One final aspect of this, it shows Matthew's hostility to Jewish rivals. This is the way in which Matthew has the taunts from the crowd at the crucifixion of Jesus echo the temptations presented Jesus by the devil. Here in 4:1-11, the devil says "If you are the son of God, if you are the son of God," and at the cross of Jesus, those passersby say,

"If you are the son of God, save yourself. If you are the son of God, come down from the cross." Is it an eerie echo, but it obviously does not cast the Jewish opponents of Jesus in a positive light. They take on a kind of demonic guise.

As we begin to move into Matthew's account of Jesus's ministry, as I've said, he follows Mark's account fairly closely, but with some interesting twists. We notice that Mark was fond of doublets, of telling similar stories twice. Matthew's even more fond. He keeps Mark's doublets, like the double feeding of the multitude, in Chapter 14:13-21, and the feeding of the 4,000 in 15:32-38, and he adds some of his own. As we saw, Jesus heals two Gergesene demoniacs and two blind men. In fact, he heals two blind men twice, so he's very fond of doublets, something that we'll see that Luke is not.

Another feature that we see is that Matthew continues to use the formula citations to show that every aspect of Jesus's life and his ministry is in fulfillment of Torah. When Jesus preaches in Chapter 8, Verse 17, Matthew notes, "This was to fulfill what was said by the prophet Isaiah, 'He took our infirmities and bore our diseases.'" I repeat, this is not in Mark; it is something added by Matthew to interpret the story. Again in Chapter 12, he tells more stories of Jesus's healings. "Jesus, aware of the fact that the Pharisees were opposing him, withdrew from there, and many followed him, and he healed them all, and ordered them not to make him known. This was to fulfill what was spoken by the prophet Isaiah: 'Behold, my servant whom I have chosen, my beloved with whom my soul is well pleased. I shall put my Spirit upon him, and he shall proclaim justice to the Gentiles.'"

Again, in Chapter 13, when Jesus tells parables, Matthew says he tells parables so that people will not understand. "With them indeed is fulfilled the prophecy of Isaiah which says: 'You shall indeed hear but never understand; you shall indeed see but never perceive. For this people's heart has grown dull, and their ears are heavy of hearing, and their eyes they have closed, lest they should perceive with their eyes, and hear with their ears, and understand with their heart, and turn for me to heal them.'" He also quotes Psalm 78 about revealing things in secret.

When Jesus enters into the city of Jerusalem, in Chapter 21, Matthew has the saying of Zechariah, Chapter 9, Verse 9, "This took place to fulfill what was spoken by the prophet, saying, 'Tell the daughter of Zion, Behold, your king is coming to you, humble, and mounted on an ass, and on a colt, the foal of an ass.'" Matthew takes that so literally that he provides both animals. Instead of regarding it as parallelism, he has both the ass and the foal of an ass that Jesus uses in his entry into the city. Matthew even has the death of Judas in fulfillment of the prophecy of Zechariah, "Then was fulfilled what had been spoken by the prophet Jeremiah, 'And they took the thirty pieces of silver, the price of him on whom a price had been set by some of the sons of Israel, and they gave them for a potter's field, as the Lord had directed me.'"

From the genealogy and the careful structuring of the infancy account, to the identification of John the Baptist as Elijah, to the identification of Jesus as God's son because of his obedience in the desert, to the formula citations of Torah that stand within his narrative, Matthew shows that Jesus is not simply Messiah because of his resurrection, but he is legitimately the messiah of Israel by means of Davidic descent, Holy Spirit, obedience, and prophetic fulfillment.

Lecture Fifteen
Gospel of Matthew—Jesus and Torah

Scope:

Matthew's Gospel not only shows that Jesus's life fulfills messianic expectations as expressed in Torah, but it also shows Jesus as the definitive interpreter of Torah, as shown in his Sermon on the Mount (chs. 5–7), in his controversy stories, and in his sustained attack on rival Jewish teachers, the Scribes and Pharisees (ch. 23). Most strikingly, Matthew uses the symbols that were attached to Torah in formative Judaism to suggest that Jesus is the very personification of Torah.

Outline

I.   Matthew's Gospel is often thought of as "more Jewish," but it is actually simply more Pharisaic in its tone and concerns.

    A.   The ideals of the Pharisees and the skills of the Scribes came together after the fall of the temple to form the Judaism that would be "classical" for two millennia and, therefore, most familiar to readers today as "Jewish," but it is simply the survivor among rival groups.

    B.   The Pharisees centered themselves not in the temple (as the Sadducees did) or in the kingship (as the Zealots did) or in the purity of the land (as the Essenes did) but in the perfect observance of Torah.

        1.   They considered all Israelites to be "priests" and, therefore, obligated to obey all the commands given to priests.

        2.   Righteousness is measured by the faithful observance of God's will as expressed in the commandments. Each word of Torah is holy and normative.

        3.   Christians made a distinction between moral commandments and ritual commandments. This is contrary to the Pharisaic spirit.

    4. To observe the commandments in changing circumstances, however, a means of interpretation is required to contemporize the ancient texts (*midrash*).

  C. Within what became the "Rabbinic tradition," Torah took on a number of symbolic associations.

    1. Torah expresses the mind of God and is the blueprint for creation; when revealed on Mt. Sinai, it restores the "image of God" to humanity.

    2. Torah is, therefore, both eternal and present to humans. It is indeed the mediator of God's presence (*shekinah*).

    3. Studying the laws concerning sacrifice is as good as (or even better than) the actual sacrifices carried out in the temple.

    4. Torah is wisdom, and taking its yoke (as in observing Sabbath) is both freedom and rest.

II. There are obvious ways in which Matthew has Jesus inhabit the world of Torah in a way distinctive to his Gospel.

  A. Every moment of Jesus's existence fulfills the prophecies of Torah (see previous lecture).

  B. Jesus is the authoritative and definitive interpreter of Torah for Israel.

    1. Jesus's Sermon on the Mount (chs. 5–7) shows Jesus as revealing God's will for those who want to belong to "the kingdom of Heaven." The programmatic statement of 5:17–20 and the antitheses of 5:21–48 are particularly revealing of "the messianic interpreter."

    2. Matthew takes special pains to connect Jesus's declarations on Torah to his acts of mercy during his ministry (8:4; 9:13; 12:5–7; 12:12; 19:4; 15:1–9; 21:16).

  C. In chapter 23, Matthew has Jesus attack the Scribes and Pharisees with a sustained polemic.

    1. Note the placement of the passage between the series of controversies with Jewish leaders in chapter 22 and the eschatological discourse to insiders in chapters 24–25.

2. Matthew uses the conventional polemic used for attack among Hellenistic and Jewish rival schools to diminish the authority of opponents.

III. Most impressively, Matthew artfully suggests that Jesus even personifies Torah, making it possible to declare that Jesus is "Torah made human."

   A. In Jesus's interpretation of Torah, his use of the first-person singular, "but I say to you," is not only unprecedented in Judaism but asserts an authority equal to the God who revealed Torah. Likewise, Jesus, as was done in ancient wisdom, tells the wealthy man to find perfection by selling all and following him.

   B. Matthew has Jesus compare himself favorably to the temple (12:6), the prophet Jonah (12:41), and Solomon (12:42).

   C. In subtle fashion, Matthew uses the symbolic associations of Torah in connection with Jesus:
      1. Jesus is wisdom personified (11:19; 23:34).
      2. Jesus's words will never pass away (5:18; 24:35).
      3. Jesus is the Sabbath rest for those who take his yoke (11:28–30).
      4. Jesus is present to those gathered in his name (18:20).
      5. Jesus remains with his followers forever (28:20).

Essential Reading:

The Gospel of Matthew, 5–7 and 23.

Supplementary Reading:

A. J. Saldarini, *Matthew's Jewish-Christian Community* (Chicago: University of Chicago Press, 1994).

J. P. Meier, *Law and History in Matthew's Gospel: A Redactional Study of 5:17–48* (Rome: Biblical Institute Press, 1976).

Questions to Consider:

1. Why is it more accurate to speak of "Matthew's Sermon on the Mount" than to speak of "Jesus's Sermon on the Mount"?

2. Why is the polemic in Matthew 23 important for understanding the context of the Gospel but problematic for Jewish-Christian relations?

Lecture Fifteen—Transcript
Gospel of Matthew—Jesus and Torah

In the opening lecture on Matthew's Gospel, I mentioned that Matthew extended Mark's narrative in two directions. By including a genealogy and an infancy account, Matthew connected the story of Jesus more explicitly to the heritage of Israel, and by including explicit resurrection accounts and a final commission to the disciples, Matthew connects the story of Jesus more explicitly to the church. In these last two lectures on Matthew (and there could be many, many more), I will develop each of these connections more fully. In this lecture, I take up the link with Judaism in the topic "The Gospel of Matthew: Jesus and Torah."

I've mentioned several times that Matthew's Gospel is often thought of as more Jewish, and for that reason it was thought of as being the first Gospel written indeed by an eyewitness disciple of Jesus named Matthew, the tax collector. But in fact it is actually simply more Pharisaic Jewish in its tone and concerns. The ideals of the Pharisees, I suggested in the last lecture, and the interpretive skills of the scribes, the *sophorim*, came together after the fall of the temple to form the Judaism that would be classical for the next two millennia. Sometimes it's called rabbinic Judaism, sometimes Talmudic Judaism, sometimes even normative Judaism, and since it endured over two millennia, it is most familiar to us today as recognizably Jewish, so we find the same kinds of concerns and convictions that are in Matthew's Gospel along conservative and especially orthodox Jews today, so it isn't more Jewish; it is simply Pharisaic Jewish, which is the survivor among rival groups in Judaism before the fall of the temple.

The Pharisees center themselves not in the temple, like the Sadducees, or in the kingship, like the Zealots, or in the purity of the land, like the Essenes, but in the perfect observance of Torah, God's commandments, the *Mitzvot,* that are revealed in the Law of Moses. With the fall of the temple, the other competitive groups within Judaism fell away. The temple disappears, the land is occupied by the

Romans, there's no possibility of a king, but Torah endures forever. Let me talk about three central convictions of the Pharisees, which were put into action through the interpretive skills of the scribes.

First, the Pharisaic group, which is called a *chabura,* or fellowship, was an intentional community; one decided to be a Pharisee, and the name apparently means separate or apart, so it's an intentional group that is very decisive in its commitments. They considered all Israelites to be priests. In other words, they did not regard the commandments of God that dealt with the priesthood and the temple, Aaron and his sons who performed sacrifices, as any less mandatory on all Israelites as the other commandments. They made no distinction between who is a priest and who is not. At some level one could talk about this as a priesthood of the laity or priesthood of the people. So they found that all of the commandments in Torah were obligatory for all Jews, and they committed themselves to that. That's how they were Pharisees. The laws of purity, the laws of tithing, the laws of diet, the laws of observance of the Sabbath, all of these were required of all Jews. That was their conviction.

Secondly, they regarded righteousness, or being rightly related to God within the covenant as measured by the faithful observance of God's will as expressed in the commandments, the Mitzvot. Each word of Torah therefore is holy—it's God's word—and each word of Torah is normative. Christians made a distinction between moral commandments, such as, do not kill, do not steal, do not commit adultery, do not bear false witness, and what Christians call ritual commandments, Sabbath observance, diet, purity laws, sacrificial laws. This is completely contrary to the Pharisaic spirit. There is no distinction between moral and ritual commandments. All come from God, all are holy, all are obligatory.

Indeed, the ritual commandments at some level are more worthy of being observed precisely because they are arbitrary, precisely because they do signify devotion to the one God. Thus, Sabbath, what could be more arbitrary than simply taking one day of the week and keeping it holy is precisely to be separate from others and therefore to acknowledge the oneness of God, the separateness of God, and therefore be different among other people. Thirdly, the problem is that the Torah was written long ago. It's ancient; it was written for an agricultural people, a nomadic people. Pharisees lived in big cities; they were an urban intentional community. The difficulty is adapting Torah to changing circumstances. How can you take scripture as absolutely normative and yet live it in circumstances that scripture had never envisaged?

Here is where the interpretive techniques of the scribes became important. They were the *sophorim*, the book people, and so Pharisees used what was called the oral Torah, which simply meant the use of interpretive techniques broadly called Midrash, from the word *darash*, to search out. Midrash was a means of interpretation to contemporize the laws of Torah, so Midrash when applied to specific commandments is called halakic Midrash, from the word halak, to walk, how do we walk. If it is applied to other kinds of text, it is called haggadic Midrash, so if one is simply interpreting wisdom literature or the Psalms, that would not be a commandment, that would be a form of wisdom, or Haggada. These are the central convictions.

Understandably, within what became the rabbinic tradition, because their teachers were called rabbis, my great one, Torah inevitably took on a number of symbolic associations. Torah is understood as expressing the very mind of God. Indeed, Torah is co-eternal with God. It is the blueprint for creation. God created the world on the blueprint that was Torah, and therefore when the Torah is revealed on Mount Sinai to Moses, it restores the image of God in humanity. The idea is that when humans sinned, they blemished that image of God that God intended, and so Torah restores people to their full humanity. Torah is therefore both eternal and present to humans. Indeed, Torah is the mediator of God's presence, which in this tradition is called the *shekinah*.

There's a lovely haggadic midrash on the Song of Songs, the Song of Solomon, which says, takes the verse, " My love leaps like a gazelle across the hills," and the rabbi says, "This is like the shekinah leaping from the synagogue to synagogue wherever Torah is being read," so God's presence was there when Torah was read. Indeed, we have a saying of a rabbi close to the time of Jesus that says, "Where two or three people gather and read Torah, there is the shekinah among them." God's presence is among them, and then one rabbi even said if only one person occupies himself with Torah, there the shekinah is present, so Torah mediates God's presence.

Thirdly, studying the laws concerning sacrifice was regarded as just as good or even better than the actual sacrifices carried out in the temple. Obviously, this became an even greater conviction after the fall of the temple, so that animal sacrifices are good, but what was called spiritual sacrifices, the use of the mind in studying the laws concerning sacrifice, was regarded as equally meritorious. In other words, everything that the temple gave you in blood and guts in a specific location is now portable through the process of study.

Fourthly then, Torah is wisdom. This is extremely important because it is the basis of what Hellenistic Jews called Jewish philosophy. God's commandments are not arbitrary—they show us what humans are supposed to be—and therefore, by studying them, this is a form of wisdom. Just as in the Book of Proverbs, wisdom calls out to the foolish man, come follow me, come dwell with me, as a symbol for studying God's word, so this was attributed to Torah. When a young man was bar mitzvahed, became a son of the commandment, it is said that one took the yoke of Torah upon oneself; that is, as oxen are yoked and therefore move in a certain direction, so Torah is the yoke of God's rule that one takes upon oneself, but this is not regarded as a form of slavery; it is regarded as a form of freedom, and even of rest. Remember the Sabbath day was meant to be a day of studying Torah, so it wasn't a day to play soccer or just amuse oneself. The reason why Sabbath was set apart was precisely so that one could study and enjoy Torah. That is sharing in God's own rest.

When we look at the Gospel of Matthew against this backdrop, we can see that there are some obvious ways that Matthew has Jesus inhabit the world of Torah in a way that's utterly distinctive to his Gospel and not found in any of the other Gospels. As we've already seen, Matthew has every moment of Jesus's existence fulfilling the prophecies of Torah through the use of these formula citations. Let's take that as read—we've talked about it twice already—and move on to the next point. Matthew also shows Jesus as the authoritative and definitive interpreter of Torah. It's not simply that his life fulfilled Torah; he interprets the genuine meaning of Torah. This is found especially in the Sermon on the Mount in Chapters 5-7 programmatically, so we have Jesus opening this sermon in Chapter 5 with the Beatitudes, blessed are the poor, blessed are those who mourn, blessed are the meek. . .

Remember the Book of Deuteronomy, Chapter 30, where Torah is presented to the people of Israel in terms of blessings and curses. Blessed are those who observe Torah; cursed or those who do not. Matthew presents only blessings. But we want to look in particular at Chapter 5, Verses 17-20; let me read it out loud. "Think not," Jesus says, "that I have come to abolish the law and the prophets; I have come not to abolish them but to fulfill them. For truly I say to you, till heaven and earth pass away, not an iota, not a dot, will pass from the law until all is accomplished. Whoever then relaxes one of the least of these commandments and teaches men so, shall be called least in the kingdom of heaven; but he who does them and teaches them will be called great in the kingdom of heaven. For I tell you, unless your righteousness exceeds that of the scribes and Pharisees, you will never enter into the kingdom of heaven." This is programmatic for identifying Jesus as the definitive interpreter of Torah.

What does Matthew mean by keeping these commandments? He means not keeping the commandments the way the Pharisees interpreted them but keeping the commandments the way Jesus interpreted. These commandments I am now giving you are the ones that are not going to pass away. Notice the point of comparison. Unless your righteousness exceeds that of the scribes and the Pharisees, you can't be part of God's rule, so Jesus is presented here as this definitive messianic interpreter of Torah. What follows, you will notice in this sermon, are a series of what are called antitheses. "You have heard that it was said to the men of old, `You shall not kill; and whoever kills shall be liable to judgment.' But I say to you that every one who is angry with his brother shall be liable to judgment; whoever insults his brother shall be liable to the council, and whoever says, `You fool!' shall be liable to the fire of hell."

Then again in 27, "You have heard it said, 'You shall not commit adultery.' But I say to you that every one who looks at a woman lustfully has already committed adultery in his heart." Verse 31, "It was also said, 'Whoever divorces his wife, let him give her a certificate of divorce.' But I say to you, no divorce." Verse 33, "You have heard it was said to the men of old, 'You shall not swear falsely.' I say to you, Don't swear at all." Verse 38 "You have heard that it was said, 'An eye for an eye and a tooth for a tooth.' I say to you, Don't resist the evil one." Verse 43, "You have heard that it was said, 'You shall love your neighbor and hate your enemy.' I say to you, Love your enemies and pray for those who persecute you."

People often talk about Jesus's interpretation of Torah as internalizing, but this is only one dimension. It only applies in the case of anger and of lust or of adultery, murder and adultery, but he also is stricter than many of his fellow Jews with regard to taking oaths and divorce, far stricter than contemporary Jewish teachers, and more radical, no resistance to evil but turn the other cheek; love not only your neighbors but also your enemies. What we have here, notice, and most intriguing in terms of literary aspects, is that this is in fact the very pattern by which rabbis taught. You begin with the text of scripture and then you provide an interpretation, so Matthew has Jesus begin with "It was written, do not commit adultery, but I say to you this." So we have the form of a kind of midrashic interpretation of scripture. The difference is that Jesus does not quote other teachers, as rabbis would do. He says, "I say to you," which is quite an extraordinary position; that is, the Messiah is the definitive interpreter of scripture.

When we move from the Sermon on the Mount into Matthew's ministry, we see that Matthew takes special pains to connect Jesus's declarations on Torah to the various dimensions of his ministry of mercy. For example, in Chapter 9, Verse 13, after Jesus is challenged by people for eating with tax collectors and sinners, and the Pharisees challenge him and say to his disciples, "Why does your teacher eat with tax collectors and sinners?" (Tax collectors and sinners were people who weren't law-observant) Jesus answered, "Those who are well have no need of a physician but those who are sick." That same statement is found in Mark. It is the sick who need a physician.

Distinctive to Matthew is this line, "Go and learn what this means. I desire mercy and not sacrifice." Jesus rebukes the Pharisees for not understanding the scripture. He tells them, go read scripture, go read the prophet Hosea. I desire mercy and not sacrifice and you will better understand.

Again, in Chapter 12, Jesus is challenged when he is plucking grains of wheat on the Sabbath with his disciples. Once more, the Pharisees challenge him for breaking the law. Notice how Matthew has Jesus respond. "Have you not read in the law how on the Sabbath the priests and the temple profane the Sabbath and are guiltless? I tell you something greater than the temple is here." This is exactly what the Pharisees were claiming; something greater than the temple was here, namely, the way in that we interpret Torah and keep it, but Matthew has Jesus trump them. They don't really keep Torah properly. Notice, "And if you had known what this means, I desire mercy and not sacrifice, you would not have condemned the guiltless, for the son of man is lord of Sabbath."

Again, in Chapter 19, when we have the statement, Matthew gives us two versions of Jesus condemning divorce, one in Chapter 5 and another time in Chapter 19. And, again, it is combined with a close interpretation of scripture. In Chapter 21, Verse 16, after Jesus enters into the city, and we saw that Matthew already used the formula citation quite woodenly, the quotation from Zechariah about Jesus coming in on the ass and the foal of the ass into the city to be greeted as the one who is blessed because he comes in the name of the Lord, in Matthew, that is followed by this event.

14: And the blind and the lame came to him in the temple, and he healed them.

15: But when the chief priests and the scribes saw the wonderful things that he did, and the children crying out in the temple, "Hosanna to the Son of David!" they were indignant;

16: and they said to him, "Do you not hear what these are saying?" And Jesus said to them, "Yes; have you never read, `Out of the mouth of babes and sucklings thou hast brought perfect praise'?"

17: And leaving them, he went out of the city to Bethany and lodged there.

Notice what is happening here. Matthew not only shows us that Jesus is the new Moses sitting on the mountain interpreting Torah for his disciples but in the course of his ministry he has Jesus, when attacked by scribes and Pharisees for not keeping the law, rebut them by being a better interpreter of law than they are, so it's characteristic of Matthew to challenge them by saying have you not read. We get another window into the social world of Matthew in Chapter 23. In Chapter 23, we have an extended attack by Jesus on the scribes and Pharisees. It's a very striking passage, not least because of the way in which Matthew has edited this.

This is Q and M material. The Q material attacking scribes and Pharisees is also found in the Gospel of Luke, Chapter 11, but Matthew has put it together in a very specific way. First, let's look at its placement. Recall Mark. In Mark, Jesus engaged his opponents in controversy in Chapter 12 in the precincts of the temple and then withdrew in Chapter 13 to give the apocalyptic discourse to his disciples. Matthew inserts this polemical attack on the scribes and Pharisees right in between those two passages, so what we have is a series of controversies, and then Jesus turns to his followers and says, "Don't pay any attention; don't imitate those people," so Matthew expands the distance between Jesus and the Pharisees and the scribes before turning in Chapter 24 to give his disciples the eschatological discourse; so the simple placement of this chapter is fascinating.

Matthew has Jesus tell his disciples and the crowds, "The scribes and the Pharisees sit on Moses's seat; so practice and observe whatever they tell you, but not what they do; for they preach, but do not practice." This is the classic charge made by philosophers against false philosophers in antiquity. It's not that the scribes and the Pharisees are wrong, notice, to teach Moses; what's wrong is that they don't really do it. What follows in Chapter 23 is the classic form of ancient polemic against false teachers. They do everything simply for show. They are hypocrites; they are blind guides. These are all standard charges made against rivals, and it indicates to us precisely that Matthew's community was in the position of a rival community with formative Judaism shaped by Pharisees and scribes.

Right in the middle of this attack, we have this. "But you are not to be called rabbi, for you have one teacher, and you are all brethren. And call no man your father on earth, for you have one Father, who is in heaven. Neither be called masters, for you have one master, the Christ. He who is the greatest among you shall be your servant; whoever exalts himself will be humbled, and whoever humbles himself will be exalted." Most impressively, Matthew artfully suggests that Jesus not only fulfills Torah and interprets Torah, but that he even personifies Torah, so that it would be possible to declare that Jesus is Torah made human. Here I'll remind you of the way in which Jesus interprets Torah, his use of the first person singular, "but *I* say to you." This is completely unprecedented within Judaism.

In fact there's a famous story about Rabbi Hillel who went off and learned all kinds of rules of argumentation in Babylon, came back, entered into the group of fellow Pharisees and scribes—they're reading a hard passage of scripture—and he says, "Here's what I think it means," and they threw him out. He came back in, "Here's what I think it means," and they threw him out. Everything has to happen three times, of course. He comes back the third time and he says "This is what I heard from my teacher, who heard it from his teacher, who heard it from his teacher, who heard it from Moses on Mount Sinai," and they said, "Now we'll listen to you." The entire rabbinic tradition is based upon this deference to authority. When Matthew has Jesus say, "But I say to you," it's unprecedented because he has Jesus asserting an authority equal not to Moses but to the God who revealed Torah.

Likewise, Jesus, like ancient wisdom, tells the wealthy man that he can find perfection by selling all and following him. In Matthew's version of the rich man in Chapter 19, Verses 21-22, the man asks him "I've done all these commandments. What do I still lack?" and Jesus says to him, "If you would be perfect, go sell what you possess, give to the poor, and come follow me." Following Jesus is like following wisdom. Matthew has Jesus compare himself favorably to the temple. In Chapter 12, Verse 6, Jesus says something greater than the temple is here. He compares himself favorably to Jonah; something greater than Jonah is here in 12:41. He compares himself favorably to Solomon: "Something greater than Solomon is here," he says in Chapter 12, Verse 42. In other words, the temple, the prophets, and the teacher of wisdom, Jesus is greater than all of them.

Finally, in very subtle fashion, Matthew uses the symbolic associations of Torah in connection with Jesus. Jesus is wisdom personified. In Chapter 11:19, when Jesus is being attacked by others, he says, "Yet wisdom is justified by her deeds," and again in Chapter 23, Verse 34, after attacking the Pharisees and scribes, he says, "Therefore I send you prophets and wise men and scribes, some of whom you will kill and crucify." Matthew has Jesus say twice that his words will never pass away, so like Torah, they are eternal. Jesus is the Sabbath rest. This is that wonderful passage that is found only in Matthew's Gospel in Chapter 11, Verses 28-30, where Jesus cries out, "Come to me, all who labor and are heavy laden, and I will give you rest (that is, Sabbath rest). Take my yoke upon you (like the yoke of Torah) and learn from me (as you would learn from Torah); for I am gentle and lowly in heart, and you will find rest (Sabbath rest) for your souls. For my yoke is easy, and my burden is light." This is only intelligible within the frame of the symbolic world of Phariseeism.

Finally in Chapter 18, Verse 20, Jesus says, "Where two or three are gathered in my name, there I will be in the midst of them." What the rabbi said about the shekinah, when two or three are gathered by studying Torah, Jesus is made to say by Matthew applies to two or three gathered in his name. And, at the very end of Matthew's Gospel in the great commission, we see that Jesus says, "For lo, I am with you always to the close of the age." Just as Jesus is eternal wisdom, so he will be with his followers forever. In short, Matthew shows Jesus to fulfill Torah, to definitively interpret Torah, and, finally and most boldly, personify Torah. If the Gospel of John can declare of Jesus the word became flesh, Matthew, no less powerfully, shows Jesus as Torah become human.

Lecture Sixteen
Gospel of Matthew—Teacher and Lord

Scope:

The characteristic image of Jesus in Matthew's Gospel is that of the teacher. Yet Matthew's careful redaction of Mark's use of the titles "Teacher" and "Lord" as applied to Jesus shows that Jesus is understood as the risen Lord who teaches the church. No Gospel gives such explicit attention to the instruction of the church as such (see especially chapters 10 and 18). To this image of Jesus corresponds the portrayal of the disciples. As in Mark, they are morally inadequate (especially their spokesperson Peter), but because they are to "teach all that [Jesus] has commanded," they are portrayed as intelligent and understanding students.

Outline

I.   In Matthew's Gospel, Jesus is not just another teacher or rabbi but teaches as the risen Lord of the church.

   A. "Teacher" (*didaskalos*) can be applied to any human being who instructs; in early Christianity, "lord" (*kyrios*) is the title used for Jesus in virtue of the resurrection.

   B. In Mark's Gospel, no real distinction is drawn between the titles; Jesus is called teacher frequently and by everyone: disciples, the needy, and enemies.

   C. Matthew edits Mark with great care to provide a different perspective.
   1. Only outsiders designate Jesus as teacher or rabbi, and only insiders call Jesus "lord."
   2. The exceptions to this practice prove the rule (see 23:8–10; 26:25, 49).
   3. A telling exception has to do with the "insider" Judas who, at the last supper and in the garden, calls Jesus "rabbi" rather than the expected "lord."

D. The significance of this redactional activity is that Jesus teaches in Matthew's Gospel with the authority of the risen Lord, not with merely human authority as another rabbi.

II. Matthew's discourses provide genuine teaching for the church that gathers in the name of Jesus.

A. Matthew's is the only Gospel that explicitly uses the term "church" (*ekklesia*) during the ministry of Jesus (16:18; 18:17).

B. Three dimensions of life in the church emerge from Matthew's discourses.

    1. The Sermon on the Mount (chs. 5–7) and the "missionary discourse" (ch. 10) portray following Jesus in terms of a life of radical simplicity, integrity, and courage. For example, Matthew opposes Jesus's understanding of piety (as a private matter) to the caricature of the Pharisees, who do good works ostentatiously in order to be perceived as pious. The Sermon on the Mount in Matthew's Gospel is not Jesus's sermon, but one that has been constructed by Matthew. Nevertheless, it is considered to be a masterly portrayal of what Jesus was about. In chapter 10, the 12 disciples must go out in poverty to teach the Gospel. Their fate will be the same as that of Jesus.

    2. The ideals of humility and mutual service within the community are prescribed by Jesus in the discourse of chapter 18. The ideal of a community in service to children is presented. There must be mutual correction and forgiveness in this community.

    3. The church is depicted as a mixed community of the perfect and the imperfect and as a community that stands under God's judgment in Matthew's parable discourse (ch. 13) and eschatological discourse (chs. 24–25). Matthew's entire Gospel is about action rather than words — doing the works of repentance.

III. The more positive portrayal of the disciples in Matthew corresponds to his portrayal of Jesus as the teacher of the church.

   A. In Mark, the disciples were not only lacking in insight, but they were morally deficient. They neither understood nor were loyal to Jesus.

   B. In Matthew, the "twelve disciples" (10:1; 11:1; 20:17) are also morally defective, but they are intelligent.

      1. Jesus calls them "men of little faith" (6:30; 8:26; 14:31; 16:8), and they fail Jesus in his passion (26:56) and even when he is resurrected (28:17).

      2. But Matthew softens Mark's harsher characterizations (8:23–27; 9:18–26; 17:1–8), and the disciples "understand" the parables (13:10–17) and are capable of teaching others (13:51–52).

      3. The portrait of Peter corresponds to this distinction. On one side, Peter has the deepest insight into the identity of Jesus and is given authority over the church (16:16–19). On the other side, his betrayal is all the more grievous (26:69–75; see 5:34).

   C. The disciples in Matthew need to be more intelligent and understanding, because their great commission demands not only baptizing all nations, but "teaching everything that I have commanded you" (28:20).

IV. In the history of Christianity, Matthew's Gospel has been preeminently the "Gospel of the church" in two ways.

   A. It has enjoyed more liturgical usage than the other Gospels and has been given more attention by commentators and preachers.

   B. This heavy ecclesial use is no doubt due to the fact that Matthew is crafted so consciously to be useful to the messianic congregation.

Essential Reading:

The Gospel of Matthew, 10, 16–18, 24–25.

Supplementary Reading:

J. P. Meier, *The Vision of Matthew: Christ, Church, and Morality in the First Gospel* (New York: Crossroad, 1991).

Questions to Consider:

1. What difference would it make to Matthew's first readers to have Jesus designated as "lord" and not simply as "rabbi/teacher"?

2. How does the role of Peter in Matthew's Gospel exemplify the Gospel's complex presentation of discipleship?

Lecture Sixteen—Transcript
Gospel of Matthew—Teacher and Lord

In the previous session on Matthew's Gospel, we examined more closely the connection of Jesus to the tradition of Israel, and we saw that Matthew shows Jesus to have fulfilled Torah, to have definitively interpreted Torah as the messiah, and even to have personified Torah. He is a Jewish messiah in the fullest sense of the term. I want to caution us, however, that this does not mean that Matthew's community was necessarily made up completely of Jews ethnically. We notice in the final commission that the disciples are sent out to teach all nations, and that can also be translated; *ta ethne* can also be translated as the Gentiles. So Matthew's community may have been ethnically Jewish; it may have been partly Jewish and partly Gentile in its makeup.

What I'm getting at here in terms of the literary structuring of Matthew and its social context is that Matthew's readers conceived of themselves as Jews in terms of identity because they followed Torah according to the teaching of the messiah. It's a matter of identity, not of ethnicity; so much so is this the case that in Matthew, Chapter 18, Jesus is made to say that if people don't listen to you, they shall be to you as though they were Gentiles, so even if the outsiders are simply Gentiles, so Matthew's community sees itself as Jewish. So if Jesus is a completely legitimated Jewish messiah, then people who don't recognize him as such are simply blind and are led by blind guides. In this, our final session on Matthew's Gospel, I want to develop further the other strong emphasis in this particular composition, namely, the connection between Jesus and the church under the title teacher and Lord.

In Matthew's Gospel, Jesus is not just another teacher or rabbi, but teaches as the risen Lord of the church. Let me explain what I mean. The title teacher, *didaskalos*, or the Hebrew title rabbi can be applied to any human being who instructs others. It was a title used for other Jewish teachers, for other Greco-Roman teachers and philosophers. But within Christianity, the title Lord, or *kyrios*, is used of Jesus specifically with reference to the resurrection, as we saw in the second lecture in this course. Psalm 110:1,"The Lord said to my Lord, sit at my right hand," so the Lord who is God says to the Lord who is the resurrected Jesus, sit at my right hand, and Paul in I Corinthians 12:3 said nobody can declare Jesus is Lord except in the Holy Spirit, so the title of Lord really designates Jesus not during his earthly life but Jesus after his resurrection.

When we look at Mark's Gospel, we see that Mark draws no real distinction between these titles. Everybody calls Jesus teacher: the disciples, the needy who seek his help, and his enemies. In other words, he uses the title teacher indiscriminately. As for the use of kyrios, Mark basically has those who are needy using it of Jesus, but primarily in the sense of sir rather than any exalted sense. It's fascinating to look at the way in which Matthew has carefully edited Mark in this respect because Matthew has gone through Mark carefully and altered every instance to make the titles teacher and Lord fit different speakers.

In Matthew's Gospel, only outsiders designate Jesus as teacher or rabbi and only insiders called Jesus Lord. For example, in the story of the disciples with Jesus in the storm at sea, in Mark's Gospel, "Teacher, why are you sleeping?" In Matthew's Gospel, "Lord why are you sleeping?" The disciples call Jesus as Lord, whereas in Matthew's Gospel all outsiders, all of Jesus's opponents talk about teacher or your teacher. The exceptions to this rule prove it. The first exception is in Matthew 23:10, where Jesus says, "You shall not call anybody teacher for you have only one teacher, nor shall you call anybody master for you have one master who is the Messiah." In that place, he does not use the title didaskalos but a specific title he uses only here, *kathegetes*, master.

The other exception is more telling, and it has to do with Judas. Judas, as we know, was chosen to be an insider, one of the Twelve who followed Jesus. But at the last supper, when Jesus foretells that one of them will betray him, the other disciples say in turn, "Is it I Lord, kyrios?" Judas says, "Is it I, rabbi?" In the garden, when Judas comes leading those who are going to arrest Jesus, he goes up and kisses Jesus and says, "Hail, rabbi." What does this signify? The significance of this redactional activity is that Matthew wants to show us that Jesus teaches, even within this Gospel, with the authority of the risen Lord, not with merely human authority as though he were another rabbi. Anybody who calls Jesus simply teacher or rabbi has diminished his significance to the level of the scribes and Pharisees and "the synagogue down the street." For Matthew's community, Jesus is not another interpreter; he is the one who can say "But I say unto you" and definitively as God's son interpret scripture. He is the Lord.

Matthew's discourses provide a genuine teaching for the church that gathers in the name of Jesus. First thing we should notice is that Matthew's is the only Gospel that explicitly chooses the term church, *ekklesia*, during the ministry of Jesus, so it is something of a retrojection. In Chapter 16, Verse 18, Matthew has Jesus declare to Peter, when Peter confesses that he is the Messiah, "You are Peter and upon this rock (a play on the word Peter, petra)—"You are Peter and upon this rock I will build my church, ekklesia." In Chapter 18, Verse 17, when giving instructions to the community, he says, "If you are correcting somebody who does something wrong and that person does not listen to you, go tell it to the church," so the term church is used twice in Matthew's Gospel whereas it's not used in the other Gospels.

If we look at the discourses in Matthew's Gospel from the perspective of the teaching of the church, what do we find? I'd like to discuss this under three main headings. The first has to do with the Sermon on the Mount in Chapters 5-7 and the so-called missionary discourse in Chapter 10. These discourses portray discipleship, following Jesus in terms of a life of radical simplicity, integrity, and courage. Let's look first at the Sermon on the Mount in Chapters 5-7. Jesus begins teaching on the mountain with the Beatitudes, "Blessed are the poor in spirit, for theirs is the kingdom of heaven. Blessed are those who mourn, for they shall be comforted. Blessed are the meek, for they shall inherit the earth."

These are quite remarkable statements and completely not intuitive. If anything seems not to be empirically verified, it is that the meek will inherit the earth. These are rather profoundly countercultural statements, a challenge to, a way of looking at reality in which people are poor in spirit, mourn, meek, hunger and thirst for righteousness, be merciful, be pure in heart, be peacemakers. It's no wonder that Matthew's Sermon on the Mount has continued to challenge people and be taken as the epitome of Jesus's philosophy, if you will, because it so marvelously expresses what might be called the spirituality of the Christian life.

But it's not simply the beatitudes. If we look at the antitheses—in the last lecture, I looked at these from the perspective of the conversation over against Judaism—and so you have heard it said, but I say to you in terms of murder and adultery and so forth. But if we look at these from the point of view of an understanding of life, we see that Jesus's teaching here is profoundly radical. It does represent an interior rising. It's not simply the deed of adultery; it is the attitude of lust that leads to adultery. It is not simply killing; it is rather hostility that leads to killing that must be dealt with.

There is the absolutizing of God's word, no divorce, this extraordinarily high image of marriage as indissoluble, terribly unrealistic as all human experience shows us, but nevertheless it represents, twice in Matthew's Gospel, in Chapter 5 and in Chapter 19, a teaching which is deeply rigorous. Sometimes people talk as though the Sermon on the Mount relaxed the law—it's just the opposite; it intensifies it and makes it absolute—likewise, no swearing of oaths. It's fascinating as Christians read these things that they tend to focus upon not the statements that are more absolutizing and more radical but rather the things with which people have more problems, namely, anger and sex, and those are the things that get the attention, not "Do not resist evil."

So we've seen that again this is a radical simplicity of life, a deeply counterintuitive sort of way of living, and it goes on further. After the antitheses, Jesus takes up the issues of piety, giving alms, praying, fasting, as instructions to Matthew's church. Once more, notice that each of these instructions emphasizes doing them not in public for other people to see them, but to do them in private because your father who sees in secret will reward you. Once more, we can talk about this in two ways.

At one level, Matthew is clearly opposing Jesus's understanding of piety to the caricature of Pharisaic piety in Chapter 23, because what did we see in Chapter 23 in that polemic? They do things in order to be seen by others; they are hypocrites. But if you give alms in secret, if you pray in secret, if you fast and nobody knows you're fasting, but if you anoint your face and comb your hair and wear your best clothes, then you were doing and not to be perceived as pious but rather in order to please God, and God will reward you. Matthew goes on beyond piety to the use of possessions in 6:19, following the sharing of possessions, not to serve God and mammon, not to care about the body in Chapter 6, Verses 25-33, not to be anxious about one's life. Then he moves into the relationships of mutual judgment, prayer, again, and finally entering by the narrow gate.

The Sermon on the Mount in Matthew's Gospel is not, as I have suggested, Jesus's sermon. It is constructed by Matthew. But from the time of St. Augustine on through Luther up until today, the Sermon on the Mount in Matthew is rightly considered to be one of the masterpieces of expression of who Jesus was and what Jesus's teaching is. Matthew may have been getting it, but he got a right. Likewise in Chapter 10, if we look in Chapter 10, we see that Matthew has constructed a discourse which is in the context of sending out the Twelve to heal the sick, to raise the dead, and to proclaim the kingdom of heaven, cleanse lepers, cast out demons and so forth.

Once more, if we look at this in 10:5 following, note that they are to go out without possessions. They are to go in poverty, to live a radical lifestyle, to depend upon the hospitality of others, to expect persecution, not to fear when they are in a situation of persecution, and to understand from the beginning that what has happened to Jesus will also happen to them. "The one who receives you receives me, and the one who receives me, receives the one who sent me," so there is this identification between the fate of the disciples and Jesus's fate. Matthew does it differently than in Mark, but it's the same point.

Let's look next at another dimension of the life of the church, which is found in the discourses of Chapter 18, in particular—this is the notion of the church as a place of humility and mutual service. This discourse begins with that dispute, taken over from Mark among the disciples concerning who is the greatest in the kingdom of heaven. In this discourse, Jesus presents the child as the model of being great in the kingdom of heaven, and that scandal or hurting a child is the worst of all things that people can do. If anybody hurts one of these little ones, or despises one of these little ones, one has truly offended God. Matthew has Jesus say, "It is not the will of my father who is in heaven that any one of these little ones should perish."

Then he shifts to the theme of mutual correction within the community, and here is where he uses that word "church." If somebody is at fault, go and correct them. If they do not listen, take one or two others and try to confront them. If they don't listen even to you all, then tell it to the church, and if he refuses to listen even to the church, let him be to you as a Gentile and tax collector. Whatever you bind on earth will be bound in heaven. Whatever you loose on earth will be loosed in heaven. This is the authority found within the community.

Finally, just as there is mutual correction, so must there be mutual forgiveness within the community, Chapter 18. Verses 23-35, the famous parable of the servant who is released of his debts and then goes out and beats a fellow servant who owes him something, and it's a teaching on the need for forgiveness. In 5-7 and in Chapter 10, we have this radical commitment to simplicity of life and courage. In Chapter 18, we have the ideal of a community which is in service to the little ones, in which leadership is a matter of simplicity, in which there is mutual correction but also mutual forgiveness.

The third dimension of the community is found in Chapter 13 and in Chapter 24 and 25, largely through parables. Chapter 13 and 24 and 25 are where Matthew's largest collection of parables is to be found, and here Matthew depicts the community as a mixed community of the perfect and of the imperfect. It's sort of a mixed lot and as a community that stands under God's judgment in terms of whether or not one responds in a certain fashion. Look, for example, in Chapter 13. Matthew has the parable of the sower, as did Mark. But Matthew's explanation of the parable of the sower is particularly interesting. Hear then the parable of the sower. This is the interpretation, not the parable; I'm in Matthew 13:18-23. When anyone hears the word of the kingdom and does not understand it—please note that, Matthew adds the word understanding—if anybody hears it and does not understand it, the evil one comes and snatches it away, what was sown in his heart. This is what was sown along the path.

> As for what was sown on rocky ground, this is he who hears the word and immediately receives it with joy, yet he has no root in himself but endures for a while, and when tribulation or persecution arises on account of the word immediately falls away. As for what was sown among thorns, this is the one who hears the word, but the cares of the world and the delight in riches choke the word and it proves unfruitful. As for the one who is sown on good soil, this is he who hears the word and understands it. He indeed bears fruit and yields in one case a hundredfold, in another sixty-, in another thirty-.

I want you to notice two things here. The first is that Matthew individualizes the response. It is the individual person's response, and it is calibrated in terms of understanding. If you really understand the word and do what the word commands, then you will bear fruit.

But this is not the only parable that has to do with human response. Notice that Matthew adds a parable of the tares among the wheat or the weeds among the wheat in Chapter 13, Verses 24-30. Notice what happens. The farmers discover that there are weeds among the wheat, and they come to the master and say, "Do you want us to go and gather them?" and he said "No, lest in gathering the weeds you root up the wheat together with them. Let both grow up together until the harvest. And at harvest time, I will tell the reapers, 'Gather the weeds first and bind them in bundles to be burned, but gather the wheat into the barn.'" Notice the theme of judgment. Notice the theme that within the field, wheat and weeds are going to grow up together, so the community is one that is not totally perfect. It is one in which people do make mistakes; you do have to correct them. It is one in which one makes mistakes and needs to be forgiven, and it is God's judgment in the end that will sort it out, as we say.

This is not even the last of these. Look at Chapter 13, Verse 47. Again, the kingdom of heaven is like a net that was thrown into the sea and gathered fish of every kind. "When it was full, men drew it ashore and sat down and sorted the good into the vessels, but threw away the bad, so it will be at the close of the age. The angels will come out and separate the evil from the righteous and throw them into the furnace of fire. There men will weep and gnash their teeth." So the community does what is called a *corpus mixtum*. It's a mixed body of the good and the evil; it will grow up together. God will sort it out in the end.

In Chapter 13, we have this image and this is made even more emphatic in Chapter 25. As we noted, Matthew's eschatological discourse, which is about the future time and the future judgment, is in Chapter 24, the equivalent of Mark, Chapter 13. But Matthew doesn't stop there. He adds parables. The parable of the ten maidens at the wedding, five of them are foolish, five of them are wise. Five of them get to go into the wedding; five do not. He tells a parable of the talents about the man who goes away and gives different servants different amounts of money to work with. How they respond, what they do with the money, determines whether or not they are rewarded or punished.

Finally, we have the most impressive scene in the Gospel of Matthew, namely, the final judgment, when the son of man comes on the clouds of heaven and he sits and he judges all humankind, and he separates the sheep from the goats. Notice the basis of the separation. The son of man says to the righteous, "I was hungry and you gave me to eat. I was thirsty and you gave me to drink. I was naked and you gave me clothing. I was in prison and you visited me." "Lord, when did we see you that way?" "Whenever you did it to the least of these little ones, you did it to me."

The unrighteous, "When I was thirsty, you didn't give me to drink. When I was hungry, you didn't give me to eat." "Lord, can't blame us, we didn't see you." "Whenever you did not do it to the least of these little ones, you did not do it to me." In Matthew's Gospel, it's not a matter of saying, "Lord, Lord"; it's a matter of doing the deed, of walking the walk. From John the Baptist to the final judgment,

Matthew's Gospel is entirely about doing the works of repentance, which has to do with the care for the little ones.

Let's turn finally here to Matthew's portrayal of the disciples, because Matthew's portrayal of the disciples corresponds to his portrayal of Jesus as the teacher of the church. In Mark's Gospel, as we saw, the disciples were not only stupid, if we can say that, lacking in insight; they were morally deficient. They neither understood Jesus nor, more grievously, were they loyal to him. They all fell away. What do we see in Matthew's Gospel? In Matthew, the 12 disciples, as he is fond of calling them, are also morally defective, but they are smart. They are intelligent. Let's examine this for a moment. They are not adequate morally. Jesus calls them men of little faith, and they fail Jesus in his passion, and even some of them continue to doubt after he's been resurrected, as we see in Chapter 28, Verse 17.

But Matthew softens some of Mark's harsh characterizations. Look, for example, at Chapter 9, Verse 18-26, the healing of the woman with the hemorrhage, and compare it to the same version in Mark. In Mark's Gospel, the woman touches Jesus, and Jesus said, "Who touched me?" and the disciples say, "You're surrounded by this crowd, and you ask who touched you?" Not a flattering comment on the disciples, but Matthew eliminates that completely. Likewise, in the transfiguration story, we saw that in Mark, Peter responds, "Let's make three tents, one for you, one for Moses, one for Elijah," and Mark notes he did not know how to answer, for he was afraid. Notice in Matthew's version, Peter said to Jesus, "Lord, it is well that we are here," Lord, not teacher, "Lord, it is well that we are here." If you wish, I will make three booths by your leave; he says nothing about fear.

When the disciples heard the voice from heaven, they were filled with awe, but Jesus came and touched them saying, "Rise and have no fear." In other words, Matthew works hard to soften the rough edges of the disciples. But, more significantly, the disciples are intelligent. Remember when we read the interpretation of the parable, the sower? It was understanding that counted. At the end of Chapter 13, when Jesus finishes his parables, he asks his disciples, "Have you understood all this?" and they said to him, "Yes," and Matthew does not contradict that. The disciples understand Jesus's parables, they understand his teaching, and Jesus responds, "Therefore, every scribe who has been trained for the kingdom of heaven is like a householder who brings out of his treasure what is new and what is old." In other words, they are now like the scribes in the Pharisaic tradition: they understand Jesus; they are capable of interpreting Jesus and teaching others.

The portrait of Peter in Matthew's Gospel corresponds to this distinction. On one side, Peter has the deepest insight into the identity of Jesus and is given authority over the church. "You are Peter and upon this rock I will build my church." This is found in Matthew 16:16-19. But on the other side, Peter's betrayal is all the more grievous because of his great insight. He had understanding; he didn't have the moral fortitude. And so when Peter denies Jesus, notice that Matthew adds, "Peter took an oath and said, 'I do not know the man.'" In other words, Jesus, who forbade taking an oath in Matthew 5:34, Peter is clearly here disobeying what Jesus said.

Why did the disciples need to be intelligent? Because then are sent by Jesus not only to baptize all nations but to teach them to observe all that I have commanded you. To be good teachers, they need to be intelligent. So in the history of Christianity, Matthew's Gospel has preeminently been the Gospel of the church in two ways. It has enjoyed more liturgical use, it's read more, commented on more by preachers, by interpreters, but that heavy ecclesial use obviously owes something to the fact that Matthew is consciously crafted to be useful to messianic congregations.

Lecture Seventeen
Luke-Acts—The Prophetic Gospel

Scope:

The Gospel of Luke and the Acts of the Apostles form a single literary composition in two volumes that can properly be called, "Luke's Gospel." Although the first volume concerns Jesus and the second volume, the early church, Jesus continues as a character and Luke portrays the church as continuing Jesus's work. This presentation discusses the implications of reading the two volumes as a single work, with particular attention to the way in which Luke uses geography and prophecy as literary devices.

Outline

I. The Gospel ascribed to Luke consists of a two-volume composition conventionally designated Luke-Acts.

  A. The Gospel of Luke (the first volume) tells the story of Jesus by using Mark as his main narrative source and discourse material from Q and L.

   1. Like Matthew, Luke follows the Markan storyline from baptism to burial, but Luke follows Mark even more closely than Matthew, altering Mark's language mainly for correctness and clarity.

   2. Luke omits a substantial portion of Mark's middle section (Mark 6:45–8:26), probably out of a dislike for doublets and a concern for the portrayal of Jesus and the disciples.

   3. Luke adds narrative material at the beginning with infancy accounts (chs. 1–2) and at the end with several appearance stories and an account of the ascension (ch. 24).

   4. Luke adds a substantial amount of Q material (shared with Matthew) and L material, most notably, the distinctive Lukan parables.

5. Luke exploits a narrative seam in Mark—Jesus's journey to Jerusalem—and expands it to include the bulk of his discourse material (Luke 9–19).

6. Luke adds a prologue to each of his volumes, that in the Gospel (1:1–4) being the most significant.

B. The Acts of the Apostles (the second volume) tells the story of the early church, with special attention to Peter (chs. 1–12) and Paul (chs. 13–28).

1. Luke appears to be the first to undertake this narrative; if he had written sources, they are undetectable.

2. He therefore had greater freedom in the construction of the narrative, and like Hellenistic historians, used journeys, speeches, and summaries, to flesh out the few facts available to him.

C. The genre that best fits Luke-Acts as a whole is that of history, but it is important to recognize that the volumes together form "Luke's Gospel."

1. The literary implication of the two-volume work is that Acts represents not only an extension but also an interpretation of the first volume.

2. The theological implication is that the story of the church continues the story of Jesus. Luke links them by a variety of means, but most importantly by having the same Holy Spirit at work in Jesus also at work in his followers.

II. Luke uses geography as a way of focusing attention on the critical part of his narrative.

A. The Gospel narrative tends toward the city of Jerusalem (2:22; 2:41–51; 4:9; 9:31, 51; 13:22; 19:11, 28).

B. The narrative in Acts moves out from Jerusalem (1:8) but constantly circles back to the city.

C. Luke thereby makes the reader focus on events in Jerusalem that form the middle of the story (Luke 19–Acts 8): Here, Jesus is rejected, raised, exalted, and here, his disciples are empowered to preach and heal in his name.

III. An even more important literary device spanning both volumes is Luke's use of prophecy.

    A. As in the other Gospels, Luke notes the way that the events in his story stand in "fulfillment" of prophecies written in Torah, although he avoids Matthew's formula citations and extends such fulfillment to the events of Acts, as well.

    B. More distinctive is the way in which characters in the narrative make statements that are prophetic and that are "fulfilled" by the subsequent events in the narrative.

        1. Sometimes, this is a matter of a "self-fulfilling prophecy" within a single incident (Jesus in Nazareth, Stephen's martyrdom).

        2. Sometimes, it is a matter of "programmatic prophecy," in which a statement governs the direction of the subsequent narrative.

    C. Luke also portrays his major characters as prophets in the tradition of Moses.

        1. In the Gospel, Jesus is portrayed as a prophet who brings God's visitation to the people.

        2. In Acts, all the protagonists are depicted in prophetic terms.

    D. Each of the Synoptic Gospels engages a distinct aspect of the symbolic world of Torah: Mark uses apocalyptic; Matthew, rabbinic; and Luke, prophetic dimensions of contemporary Judaism.

IV. Luke is distinctive by prefacing each of his volumes with a prologue.

    A. The prologue to Acts is a simple connective to the first part of the story.

    B. The prologue to the Gospel (Luke 1:1–4) serves as an important interpretive clue to Luke's religious purposes.

        1. He is writing a certain sort of history, about the fulfillment of God's promises.

        2. He writes his story in sequence to provide assurance to his Gentile readers.

Essential Reading:

The Gospel of Luke and the Acts of the Apostles.

Supplementary Reading:

L. T. Johnson, *The Writings of the New Testament*, pp. 213–257.

H. J. Cadbury, *The Making of Luke-Acts* (New York: Macmillan, 1927).

Questions to Consider:

1. How does the decision to read all of Luke-Acts as the "Gospel According to Luke" affect the way the two volumes are interpreted?

2. Why does "prophecy" best describe Luke's distinctive way of engaging the symbolic world of Torah—in contrast to Mark and Matthew?

Lecture Seventeen—Transcript
Luke-Acts—The Prophetic Gospel

Over the next four lectures, we will be considering by far the most substantial effort at Gospel composition in the f[st] century, the good news according to Luke. Following the two-source hypothesis, of the solution to the synoptic problem, we envisage this composition, like Matthew's Gospel, as composed at some point long enough after the writing of Mark to have allowed that Gospel to circulate and to be used by the authors of Matthew and of Luke, therefore conventionally dated around the year 85, but that date is largely a matter of guesswork. The author of this composition could be Luke the physician, the companion of Paul, but need not be, and we certainly cannot derive any interpretive perspective on the Gospel from that putative authorship. As always, we will approach this composition through its literary shape and try to reach conclusions about its situation and what issues it's trying to address from the way in which it is put together.

We can begin our analysis with the same kind of redactional approach we used with Matthew, mainly, with the way that the Gospel of Luke uses the Gospel of Mark. The Gospel of Luke actually consists of a two-volume composition, conventionally designated Luke-Acts. Although most people think only of the first when they think of Luke's Gospel, it is clear that the author intended both the gospel portion, the first volume, and the second volume, which we call the Acts of the Apostles to be read as a single composition, as his version of the good news. The first volume uses the Gospel of Mark, as Matthew used Mark, as the main narrative source that Luke uses to construct his gospel story into which he infuses substantial additions of discourse material drawn from Q, the material he shares with Matthew, and L, the material that is distinctive to Luke.

Like Matthew, Luke follows the Markan storyline from baptism to burial, what I have referred to as the Markan spine, that basic plot of Jesus and his disciples from the baptism of John to the burial of

Jesus. But Luke follows Mark much more closely than Matthew does. He makes far less massive changes to the diction and sentence structure and so forth of Mark's Gospel. He mainly corrects Mark's language for clarity. For example, in Luke's version of the Gadarene demoniac, in Luke 8:22-39, we see that unlike Matthew, who, you'll recall, had changed it to two demoniacs who were exorcised by Jesus, Luke follows Mark's story very carefully, including all the detail about the demoniac. But he corrects tiny details.

For example, whereas Mark says that Jesus crossed the Sea of Galilee, Luke, who had been on the Mediterranean, changes it from sea to lake. Whereas in Mark's Gospel we could have the impression that Jesus got out of the boat before he reached land, Luke makes sure that he reaches land, then gets out of the boat. Whereas in Mark's Gospel people come from a city to see what had happened when Mark had not established that the demoniac had been near a city, Luke takes pains to not introduce an unanticipated factor by having the man be in the tombs outside the city; so that he does these kinds of small corrections to Mark for correctness and clarity.

Second observation with regard to Mark is that Luke omits a substantial portion of Mark's middle section, namely, Mark 6:45 to 8:26. It's not entirely clear why he omits this material, but he probably did it deliberately. It's very unlikely that he had a version of Mark unlike the one we had that didn't have those materials. It's more likely that he simply refrained from including that material. I can think of three reasons why. The first is that although Matthew loves doublets, Luke doesn't, so Luke would not see any reason why we should have a feeding of 5,000 and then shortly thereafter a feeding of 4,000. That's simply a redundancy for Luke.

Secondly, we notice when we read Mark that there are two miracles of Jesus, two healings in this section of Mark in which Jesus appears suspiciously like a thaumaturge, like a magician, using spit and foreign languages in order to heal the deaf-mute and the blind man. Luke is so suspicious of magic being associated with Jesus that he could well have refrained from including those stories. Finally, you will recall that in this portion of Mark's Gospel, the disciples of Jesus appear as unfailingly stupid. They don't understand anything of what Jesus is up to. Again, Luke has a different perspective on the disciples, he has other ends in view for the disciples, and so these three reasons, his dislike of doublets, the image of Jesus and the image of the disciples may well account for what is called Luke's great omission of Mark's material.

Luke also adds substantial narrative material. Like Matthew, he adds an infancy account at the beginning of his Gospel, Chapters 1-2, and at the end of his Gospel he has several explicit appearances of Jesus to his followers, the marvelous story of Jesus appearing anonymously to two followers on the road to Emmaus. They do not recognize him until he breaks bread with them and then they recognize that he is Jesus, and then another appearance to the eleven disciples together. Both of these accounts, notice, involve eating, the eating of the risen lord Jesus. It's a major theme in Luke's Gospel, table fellowship, which we will see extends also into the Acts of the Apostles. Luke's Gospel ends with a very short account of the ascension of Jesus. Jesus departs from the disciples and goes into heaven. That is repeated in the Acts of the Apostles, Chapter 1, Verses 9-11, so Luke has actually two versions of an ascension account.

Like Matthew, Luke also adds a substantial amount of Q material, the stuff he shares with Matthew, mostly in the form of sayings, and L material, distinctive to his own Gospel. In addition to the narrative material he adds, what Luke contributes from his own source (And was it really a source or did he write this stuff? It's impossible to tell), but the thing that strikes us most about what Luke adds are his marvelous parables of Jesus. Many of the most striking parables ascribed to Jesus are found only in the Gospel of Luke. The publican and the Pharisee who go up to pray, the prodigal son and the elder son, Lazarus and the rich man, the good Samaritan, the unjust steward, the widow and the unrighteous judge, all of these vivid stories that we associate with Jesus, note, are found in Luke's Gospel and only in Luke's Gospel. They are L material.

Where does Luke put all of this additional discourse material? He uses a literary technique quite different than Matthew. You will recall that Matthew took all of his Q and M material and he created these great blocks of discourses, these five great lectures that stud his narrative and make Matthew so difficult to read as a story. Luke follows a very different technique. Luke takes great pains to insert the sayings of Jesus in biographically verisimilitudinous settings. He has to create room for them, however, and he does this by exploiting a tiny scene in Mark's Gospel right after the transfiguration. Before Jesus reaches Jerusalem, Mark indicates that Jesus is on a journey to Jerusalem.

In Mark, it only takes a chapter or less. Luke takes that scene and opens it up like an accordion and inserts all of this material of Jesus discoursing. Chapters 9-19 is Luke's great journey narrative, and it is his literary invention. Jesus is on the road, he's gathering disciples, he's teaching, he's sitting at table, but this is his way of including this massive amount of material, notice without losing the character of the story, so that, in effect, one reads this with the sense that there is a powerful and dynamic story going on even though Jesus is talking all the time. This is part of Luke's literary mastery.

Finally, in terms of content, Luke adds a prologue to each of his volumes. That which begins the Book of Acts is a very short, three-verse summary of the Gospel, and we'll look at that later in this presentation. The prologue to the Gospel in Chapter 1, Verses 1-4, is far more significant, and again we will look at that at the end of this particular lecture. So Luke has shortened Mark by omitting material, then he has greatly extended Mark. He's created a journey within the middle of the story in which he's inserted things: he's added infancy accounts, he's added resurrection accounts, he's added an ascension account, and finally, in his most dramatic move, he extends the Gospel by adding a complete additional volume called the Acts of the Apostles. This is the second part of Luke's work, and notice the two prologues dedicated to the same person, Theophilus, clearly indicate that these are intended to be part of the same composition.

The Acts of the Apostles then tells the story of the early church, but not as a sort of institutional, organizational, corporate development, but rather with a specific attention to certain figures who are followers of Jesus, Peter especially, in Chapters 1-12, and Paul in Chapters 13-28. As far as we can tell, Luke is the first Christian writer to undertake this part of the narrative. Nobody else had undertaken to write a narrative of what Luke calls the things that have been fulfilled among us, namely, what happens after the story of Jesus. If he had sources that he was using, they are undetectable to us. Luke is a literary artist who rewrites everything in his own style. That's why we can't tell whether it's Jesus's parables or his parables. It's all his style. If we did not have, for example, the Gospel of Mark extant, we would never be able to tell that Luke was using a source where he uses Mark. It's only because we have Mark that we're able to see that Luke used him. He so thoroughly rewrites his sources.

So as far as we can tell, he did not have sources for the Acts of the Apostles. He probably had a limited amount of material available to him, probably a handful of stories about the founding days in Jerusalem, perhaps a couple of healing stories, perhaps a couple of stories, for example, about the killing of Stephen, one of the early leaders in the church, and when he gets to Paul, he probably had some notion of Paul's itinerary, the movements of Paul across the Mediterranean world because, in fact, when we take Luke's account of Paul's journeys and put them up against Paul's letters, there are patches where they overlap each other very nicely, but, at best, he had sketchy materials with which to work.

It is important for us to recognize that Acts is largely Luke's literary invention, so that he takes a handful of facts and he renders them, if you will, fictionally, which is what all ancient historians did. They didn't have the kinds of massive documentary evidence that the biographer of a modern president would have. They basically had certain events which they then rendered in what we would now call fictional techniques. It does not mean that there is not fact beneath it, but it means that the rendering is fictional.

What are some of these techniques? Like good Hellenistic historians, Luke makes use of journeys, in the case of Jesus and in the case of Paul. It's a nice way to fill in your story by having them move in various places. Mostly, he uses speeches. If one looks carefully at Acts, you can see that, like Thucydides, Luke uses speeches everywhere as a way of telling people the significance of the story, so we have Peter giving speeches in Acts 2, in Acts 3, in Acts 10.

We have Paul giving missionary sermons in Acts 13 and 17. We have Paul's farewell discourse to the church at Ephesus in Chapter 20 and then, beginning in Chapter 21, a whole series of defense speeches that Paul makes before various venues. These speeches are a marvelous way of filling out the story.

Finally, Luke uses summaries. In Chapter 2, Verses 21-47, in Chapter 4, Verses 32-37, in Chapter 5, Verses 12-16, Luke takes individual incidents and he elevates them to the level of generality to give us the impression that what one person did, everybody was doing over an extended period of time. Thus, we have the sense in the first eight chapters of Acts, of movement, of drama, of passion, of event, but when we look carefully, we see that it's largely Luke's leisure demand as a literary artist. There's not much stuff there. It's mostly his words that create this impression of great drama. In terms of extension, this is Luke's massive work. The 24 chapters of the Gospel, the 28 chapters of Acts create the largest composition in the New Testament. It takes up fully one-quarter of the New Testament collection, so it is a large work.

If we ask the question, What kind of work is this now?—we saw what Mark was, we saw what Matthew was, but what has Luke created?—What kind of genre does it fit into in terms of ancient literature? Some have suggested that, in fact, Luke has become something like an ancient novel or the romance novels that were written in antiquity, and especially the Acts of the Apostles lends some small degree of plausibility to this because, as I said, Luke uses, perforce, fictional techniques, and so he uses the sort of techniques of storytelling that are found in Greco-Roman novels. Luke has prison escapes, strange encounters, storms at sea, shipwrecks. Did shipwrecks and storms at sea and pirates happen in the Mediterranean? You bet, and so it doesn't mean that Paul did not experience the storm in Chapter 27 of Acts and did not have a shipwreck, but Luke uses all of the literary devices in telling that story.

But clearly, Luke-Acts as a whole cannot be considered to be a novel. First of all, it has factual elements to it—as I've suggested, we can verify parts of the story substantially—but secondly, it is totally lacking, as is the whole New Testament, it totally lacks the element of the erotic. There is nothing here that approaches romance, quite differently, I should say, from later apocryphal Acts of the Apostles, such as the Acts of Paul and Thecla, which has a very strong erotic undertone. Some have suggested that Luke-Acts as a two-volume work looks like biographies of Greco-Roman philosophers. The first volume is the biography of Jesus, the founder of the school, with his teachings and his actions and his death, and the second volume is the story of his school, his successors, the apostles. That has the higher degree of plausibility, and I'll return to that in a later lecture.

For the most part, the genre in which Luke clearly fits best is that of Hellenistic history, and history of a specific kind, such as was generated both by Greco-Roman historians and Jews, called apologetic history, that is, a history which does not intend something to tell the past as it was but it tells the past as a way of defending and presenting a certain kind of identity in the world, and so Luke's is an interested history, if you will, an apologetic history for the Christian movement, yes, but I'm going to suggest that it's also, if we look at it internally, also an apologetic history in defense of God. But to get to that point, we have to move further forward.

I want to pause for a moment and remind you of the literary implications of this two-volume work called Acts. By extending the story of Jesus into the story of the church, what has Luke done? First of all, for us, it means that we can't simply compare Luke to Mark and Matthew, synoptic comparison, because by continuing the story, Luke also interprets his own story. He tells us how the story turns out, so in reading Luke-Acts, we have to read both volumes in order to get a sense of what he is up to. That's the literary implication. The theological implication is that the story of the church continues the story of Jesus. So successfully has Luke done this that for 2,000 years most Christians have simply assumed that this is a natural way to tell the story, that in fact this is the way things happened, this is the way things had to have happened.

He need not have told the story of the church at all. If he had told it, he didn't have to tell it in the fashion he did, but at every stage, Luke makes sure to show that what happens in Jesus foreshadows what happens in the church, and what happens to the apostles is intelligible only because they are connected with Jesus. We'll show this in a variety of ways; above all, he does this by showing that the same Holy Spirit which was at work in Jesus is also at work in the apostles. In this respect, Luke really is, if not a companion of Paul, a student of Paul. He has caught the deepest theological insight of Paul, which is that what was significant about the humanity of Jesus was not the historical accidents that stay in the past but rather the pattern of his existence, which is communicable to others by the Holy Spirit, and so by showing the apostles as in fact figures who resemble Jesus in their behavior, he has made a powerful theological statement.

I'd like to look at two literary devices used by Luke before we turn at the end of this class to the prologue to the Gospel. It has been recognized for a long time that Luke uses geography as a way of putting attention on the critical portion of his narrative. In the Gospel, everything moves toward the city of Jerusalem. The infancy account culminates in Jesus being presented in the temple in Jerusalem. We have the account of Jesus as a young man who is lost in the city at the feast of Passover and is found teaching in the city of Jerusalem. Luke is so obsessive about this that in the testing of Jesus, the temptation account, he changes the order of the last two testings so that the climactic one is Jesus being put on the pinnacle of the temple in Jerusalem. Again, the climax is reached in Jerusalem.

In that great journey of Jesus that begins in Chapter 9, we are reminded some 17 times by Luke that Jesus is on the way, that he's on the way. In Chapter 13:22, prophets can only die in Jerusalem, and so he constantly moves us toward Jerusalem, and once Jesus is in Jerusalem he teaches in the temple, he is arrested there, he is executed there, his resurrection appearances all take place in the neighborhood of Jerusalem, and, in fact, in the beginning of Acts, Jesus is reported as having told them, "Stay in the city," and they receive the Holy Spirit in Jerusalem, and the first church of the first eight chapters of Acts is located in Jerusalem.

The narrative in Acts moves out from Jerusalem; indeed, Jesus, in Chapter 1, Verse 8, is the resurrected Jesus. In fact, when asked, "Are you going to restore the kingdom to Israel at this time?" he says, "It's not for you to know the times and the seasons, but you are to be my witnesses. You are to receive the power from on high and you're to be my witnesses beginning in Jerusalem, Judea, Samaria, to the ends of the world," and, in effect, the risen Jesus has provided a table of contents for the Acts of the Apostles. Chapters 1-8 are in Jerusalem, then Judea, then Samaria, and then with Paul all the way to Rome, which is functionally the ends of the earth; so, in Acts, the story moves out from Jerusalem, but always circles back.

When the good news reaches Samaria, Peter and John visit and then come back to Jerusalem. When Paul goes out to do missionary work, he circles back to Jerusalem. Luke is quite deliberate, therefore, in making the reader focus on events in Jerusalem that form the middle of his story, from Luke 19 to Acts 8. Here Jesus is rejected, raised, exalted, and here his disciples are empowered to preach through the Holy Spirit and heal in his name. The movement of Luke-Acts, in other words, is centrifugal; it forces the reader's attention on this middle part of the story, which is the critical part of the story.

A second literary device that Luke uses and I'm going to develop in these lectures, is that of prophecy. As in the other gospels, Luke notes the way in which events in his stories stand in fulfillment of prophecies written in Torah. He does this mainly in speeches. But he does not use Matthew's formula citations, and he extends this fulfillment of prophecies beyond the story of Jesus into the story of the church as well. Everything that happens in Acts is also in fulfillment of prophecy. But more distinctive to Luke is the way in which characters within the narrative make statements that are prophetic and that are fulfilled by the subsequent events in the narrative.

Sometimes this happens in a rapid tick-tock, as when a character says something and it's immediately fulfilled by the succeeding narrative. Jesus says in Nazareth, "A prophet is not accepted in his own country"—boom, they don't accept him in his hometown. Stephen says, "You people are always rejecting prophets"—boom, they reject Stephen, who is a prophet. Sometimes it's a matter of programmatic prophecies in which a statement is made in one part of the narrative by a character and is fulfilled later in the narrative. I've already pointed out, Acts 1:8, Jesus makes a prophecy about them being witnesses, and the story shows in fact that it happens. Jesus's passion predictions are fulfilled in Luke's story.

The third way in which Luke uses prophecy as a literary technique is to portray his major characters as prophets in the tradition of Moses. Twice in Acts 3:22-23 and in Acts 7:35-38, Luke has characters quote Deuteronomy 18:15-16 about a prophet that God is going to raise up like Moses from among the people. Luke wants the reader to see both Jesus and his followers in Mosaic terms, as prophets like Moses, who are filled with the Holy Spirit, who speak God's word, who work signs and wonders among the people, and who generate acceptance and rejection among the people. All of the protagonists in Acts are thus presented in prophetic terms. Each of the Synoptic Gospels engages a distinct aspect of the symbolic world of Torah. We saw that Mark uses apocalyptic, Matthew uses rabbinic, and Luke uses prophetic dimensions of contemporary Judaism.

These prologues, at the end of this session I want to simply indicate the importance of, not the prologue to Acts, but the prologue to the Gospel of Luke, which serves as an important interpretive clue to Luke's religious purposes. If we look at that prologue, we can see that Luke is writing a certain kind of history about what God has brought to fulfillment among the people, and he assures Theophilus that he is writing his story in sequence (the adverb *kathexes*, in sequence) in order to provide what he calls *asphaleia*, not truth, as most translations have it, but asphalia means security or assurance about the things in which he has been instructed. In other words, Theophilus is a Christian reader who knows the story but is somewhat disturbed by aspects of the story. Luke wants to reassure him by writing the story in a certain fashion, namely, in sequence. What should be bothering a good Gentile reader, as Theophilus undoubtedly was?

The major theme in Luke-Acts is that the good news has reached the Gentiles. That moves throughout both volumes. This is God's plan from the beginning, that this good news in Jesus is going to reach all nations, not just Jews. But the dark side of that good news is that the Jews seem not to get it. They seem to reject Jesus, they seem to reject the message, and the mission among the Jews seems to have failed. The question therefore for a Gentile is, if the God of the Jews has made us God's new people, this may seem to be good news, but if you think about it a while, it's sort of like somebody who's convinced a spouse to leave their first marriage and marry them. The good news is they have a spouse; the bad news is they have a spouse who will leave a partner to marry somebody else. So if the God of the Jews has not been faithful to the Jews, this creates uncertainty among Gentiles who have now committed themselves to that God, so Luke's history is a defense of the faithfulness of God to the Jewish people.

Lecture Eighteen
Gospel of Luke—God's Prophet

Scope:

In Luke's Gospel, Jesus is presented as a prophet. He delivers a radical message of reversal of human norms in the name of God's visitation. He calls for people to repent and form a restored Israel around him. Luke shows Jesus embodying that message by a ministry of healing, both physical and spiritual. The prophet Jesus lives a radical life, characterized by itinerancy, poverty, prayer, and a servant model of leadership. He calls his followers to continue that prophetic ministry and bears witness to God's kingdom in the face of public opposition.

Outline

I. The infancy account in Luke's Gospel prepares readers to perceive Jesus as a prophet and king.

   A. Luke's infancy account (chs. 1–2) has a completely different character than Matthew's.

      1. Luke places Jesus's genealogy immediately after his baptism (3:23–38).

      2. Mary, rather than Joseph, is the main character and is given the task of interpreting events.

      3. Rather than use formula citations, Luke writes in a manner that imitates scripture.

   B. Jesus is raised among prophets; his mother, cousin, uncle and aunt, and even strangers who encounter him all utter prophetic speech concerning God's work for Israel through John and Jesus.

   C. Readers know from the beginning that the Holy Spirit is at work in Jesus (1:35, 41, 67; 2:26–27).

   D. Luke's distinctive account of the finding of Jesus in the temple (2:41–52) reveals Jesus's commitment to his Father's business.

   E. Luke's Gospel has a more biographical feel to it.

II. After his baptism and temptation, Jesus announces his prophetic vision of a restored people.

    A. The most striking feature of Luke's account of Jesus's baptism is the way in which he reveals his historical consciousness. Luke connects his story of Jesus to larger world history.

    B. John is a genuine prophetic predecessor, "proclaiming the good news" and demanding the fruits of repentance (3:1–18). Luke has John teach people about the use of possessions. This is one of Luke's major themes. For Luke, the response to God is measured by the way in which one uses one's possessions.

    C. Jesus's baptism is shaped to show him as directly and bodily receiving the Holy Spirit while in prayer (3:21–22), and the genealogy (which goes back to Adam and God) repeats the point that Jesus is the "Son of God" (3:23–38).

    D. Luke emphasizes the guiding role of the Holy Spirit through the temptation and his first teaching in Galilee (4:1, 14).

    E. Luke uses Jesus's preaching in the synagogue of Nazareth (4:16–30) to identify him as a prophetic messiah whose mission is to restore the outcast to the people, announcing a "favorable year to the Lord."

        1. Luke's account of Jesus's first sermon in his hometown of Nazareth is one of the most dramatic scenes in Luke's Gospel.

        2. In Mark's and Matthew's Gospels, the parallel account is bare.

        3. In his first sermon, Jesus announces a concept that Luke has already abundantly developed that he is anointed with the Holy Spirit and, therefore, is the Messiah.

        4. Luke uses the event of Jesus's first sermon to show that Jesus is fulfilling the prophecy of Isaiah that he is the Messiah come to proclaim good news to the poor.

        5. But, in Luke, Jesus also suffers the proverbial fate of a prophet in his own land he taunts his audience by announcing that the good news is not just for the Jews but for Gentiles, as well. On hearing this, his audience becomes enraged and rejects him.

6. Luke's version of the beatitudes and woes in his "sermon on the plain" enacts the programmatic statement in Nazareth.

7. The summary of Jesus's ministry in 7:22 reaffirms the nature of the prophet's work. The "good news" means the sick are healed, the dead are raised, and the poor have had the good news preached to them.

III. Luke portrays Jesus's ministry as a prophetic call to inclusion in God's people.

A. Luke's language about possessions has two aspects:

1. At one level, it symbolizes the marginalized of society who are called into God's favor.

2. At another level, the response to that call must be enacted by the use of possessions; that is, possessions are shared with others.

B. Physical and spiritual "healing" is at the same time a "salvation" that is social in character. Thus, in Luke, Jesus's ministry is more political than it is in Mark and Matthew; it is remarkable for the way in which Jesus reaches out to the stigmatized of society.

C. Luke uses table-fellowship as a way of symbolizing Jesus's program of healing the people. For eating with tax collectors and sinners, Jesus is rebuked by the Pharisees (7:34).

D. In Luke's narrative, sinners, the outcast, and the poor are the new righteous, while the righteous and the powerful are being excluded. The Pharisees stand as the model of those who are being excluded from the people.

E. Luke's distinctive parables serve to interpret this prophetic ministry of healing and restoration (see the Samaritan [10:29–37] and the Prodigal Son [15:11–32]).

IV. In Luke's Gospel, Jesus is himself a charismatic figure whose radical manner of life exemplifies his program.

    A. Jesus is led by the Spirit and obedient to God, as shown by his constant prayer.

    B. Jesus is poor and a wanderer who depends on the hospitality of others.

    C. Jesus exercises a form of leadership based on the service of others.

V. The Lukan Jesus calls followers to a radical discipleship that imitates the prophetic life of Jesus (see 14:26–33).

Essential Reading:

The Gospel of Luke, 1–7.

Supplementary Reading:

R. E. Brown, *Birth of the Messiah* (New York: Doubleday, 1993).

D. L. Tiede, *Prophecy and History in Luke-Acts* (Philadelphia: Fortress Press, 1980).

Questions to Consider:

1. How does Luke's thematic use of the Holy Spirit enhance his presentation of Jesus as a prophet?

2. Discuss the way in which healing is a "sign of salvation" in Luke's Gospel.

Lecture Eighteen—Transcript
Gospel of Luke—God's Prophet

We have seen some of the features of Luke's two-volume version of the good news called the Gospel of Luke and the Acts of the Apostles, or, as scholars have come to call it now, Luke-Acts, how he redacts Mark and arranges his Q and L material, how he extends the story into the second volume and thereby interprets the story of Jesus, how he uses the literary devices of geography and of prophecy. The use of prophecy, however, goes beyond a literary device for Luke. It cuts to the understanding of who Jesus is and what the good news is about. Jesus is, for Luke, God's final prophet, and the good news is a changing of the way people live in accord with that prophetic vision.

Many of us, when we hear the word prophet, think in terms of predicting the future, and, as I suggested in the last lecture, Luke does use prophecy that way. Jesus says something in the Gospel, people will bring you before synagogues and persecute you, and then that happens in the story in Acts, so there is prophecy as prediction. But in the proper Biblical sense, a prophet is more than a predictor. A prophet is a spokesperson for God, and in the Biblical tradition from Moses forward the prophet is characterized by certain features. The prophet is filled with the Holy Spirit. The prophet speaks God's words to humans. The prophet backs up that word with a lifestyle commensurate with it.

The prophet does mighty deeds among the people, so these characteristics of prophecy are the salients by which Luke is going to shape his image of Jesus and also the image of Jesus's followers. The prophet not only speaks God's word but speaks God's word as a vision of how humanity should live, and this is the way in which Luke puts together these two things. If we begin with the infancy account in Luke's Gospel, we see that he prepares readers to perceive Jesus as a prophet and as a king of Israel. Luke's infancy account, Chapters 1-2, is completely different than Matthew's. They really do not share any single story; all they share are the names of Jesus's parents and Jesus's name. Everything else is different in these two accounts.

Matthew, you'll recall, begins with a genealogy, but Luke places a genealogy immediately after Jesus's baptism in Chapter 3, Verses 23-38. Matthew had Joseph as the main character; Luke has Mary as the main character. She is the one whose faith and obedience sets the plot in motion. She is the one whose words interpret events. And rather than use formula citations, as Matthew did. Luke writes in a manner that imitates scripture. His prologue in Chapter 1, Verses 1-4, is written in good, long, periodic, complex Greek sentences.

In Chapter 1, Verse 5, Luke plunges us back in to the book of Ruth, into Biblical times. He writes in a deliberate Biblical style in order to draw imaginatively into the story of Israel. Luke presents us a series of diptychs, or a scene having to do with John the Baptist's parents, and then with Mary, a scene having to do the birth of John, and then a scene having to do with the birth of Jesus, putting John and Jesus into sort of comparison and contrast from the beginning, and these diptychs are interspersed with speeches or songs that the characters enunciate as interpretations of events, so Luke's infancy account is very distinctive.

One of the most beautiful passages in this infancy account is the song of Mary. When Mary agrees to become the mother of Jesus and her cousin Elizabeth greets her when she goes to visit her, Mary says, "My soul magnifies the Lord, and my spirit rejoices in God my Savior, for he has regarded the low estate of his handmaiden. For behold, henceforth all generations will count me blessed; for he who is mighty has done great things for me, and holy is his name." Luke has Mary imitate the song of Hannah in the first book of Samuel, so instead of using quotations from scripture, he has Mary imitate scripture, praising God for recognizing her lowliness, but notice what happens now.

Her story interprets the story of Israel, and his mercy is on those who fear him from generation to generation. He has shown strength with his arm. He has scattered the proud in the imagination of their hearts. He has put down the mighty from their thrones and exalted those of lower degree. He has filled the hungry with good things, and the rich he has sent empty away. He has helped his servant Israel in remembrance of his mercy as he spoke to our fathers, to Abraham and to his posterity forever. Mary's story of receiving the Messiah into her life is interpreted in view of God's mercy to Israel, but notice that this good news is also a reversal of human expectations. The powerful and the rich are sent away; the lonely and the poor are going to be lifted up. This is a vision that's not simply personal but political. It is a prophetic vision of what God is doing in the world, and it begins with Mary, Mary's faith, Mary's interpretation of events.

Luke shows us Jesus as enmeshed in a family of prophets; he's raised among prophets. His mother Mary speaks prophetically, his cousin John is a prophet, his uncle Zechariah speaks prophetically, his aunt Elizabeth speaks prophetically, and even strangers with whom Jesus comes into contact, the old man Simeon in the temple, and the old widow Anna in the temple. All are led by the Holy Spirit and other prophetic speech regarding God's work for Israel through John and Jesus, so when Jesus is presented in the temple, the old man Simeon, Luke says, he was:

25: looking for the consolation of Israel, and the Holy Spirit was upon him.

26: And it had been revealed to him by the Holy Spirit that he would not see death before he had seen the Lord's Christ.

27: And inspired by the Spirit he came into the temple; and when the parents brought in the child Jesus, to do for him according to the custom of the law,

28: he took him up in his arms and blessed God and said,

29: "Lord, now lettest thy servant depart in peace, according to thy word;

30: for mine eyes have seen thy salvation

Notice, he was looking for the consolation of Israel, he took the child into his arms, and he now says this is it, this is the salvation of Israel, the salvation "which thou hast prepared in the presence of all peoples, a light of revelation to the Gentiles, and for glory of thy people Israel." Luke tells the story in reverse order. Jesus is the glory of Israel in the Gospel and a light to the Gentiles in Acts. Simeon's words of prayer are words of prophecy, not simply to Jesus's parents but to the reader of Luke-Acts.

Notice that he looks at Mary, Jesus's mother, and he says, "Behold, this child is set for the fall and rising of many in Israel, for a sign that is spoken against so that the thoughts of many hearts may be revealed." In other words, Jesus is a prophet who is going to create division within the people and reveal the thoughts of people, so Luke uses these songs as prophecies for what is going to happen in Jesus and in the stories, so readers know from the beginning that the Holy Spirit is at work in Jesus, the Holy Spirit comes upon Mary when the angel Gabriel announces that she's going to give birth to the child. The Holy Spirit comes upon Elizabeth, upon Zechariah, and we saw repeatedly, Luke says, that the spirit led Simeon and filled him with the Holy Spirit so that he could speak prophetically.

All of this takes place in the first two chapters and then concludes with Luke's distinctive account of the finding of Jesus in the temple, in Chapter 2, Verses 41-52, that reveals Jesus's commitment to his father's business, and here this wonderful account which, of course, Jesus is 12, which is the age of bar mitzvah in Judaism, the entry into adulthood, so it's not really a childhood story; it's really an adolescent adulthood story. It shows us Jesus and his parents totally enmeshed in the world of Judaism.

They are law-observant; they do what is required. They go up in the feast of Passover to the city. But at the same time, it shows Jesus as transcending his family and transcending Judaism. He must be about his father's business, and so we see this sense of vocation already in that incident, so that we have the young man Jesus, if you will, with a sense of prophetic vocation. He is to represent God in the world and not simply be a carpenter in Nazareth. You see how Luke's story has a more biographical feel to it. He has a family, he's enmeshed in the family, he has an infancy, he has a young manhood, and so Mark's abrupt beginning is filled out biographically by Luke.

Let's look at the baptism and temptation account in Luke. For each of the Gospels, we have paid particular attention to the opening of Jesus's ministry as revealing something important about how this particular evangelist is working. The first thing that strikes us in Chapter 3, Verses 1-2, of Luke's version is the way in which he shows the historical consciousness. In the 15th year of the reign of Tiberius Caesar, Pontius Pilate, being governor of Judea, Herod, being tetrarch of Galilee, and so forth, Matthew and Mark were not in the least interested in connecting the story of Jesus to larger world history. Luke has that interest; he is showing us that this is not only a story about Jesus and his disciples, it's also a story about the world and with implications for the world.

In his portrayal of John, notice that John is himself a genuine prophetic figure: the word of God came to John, the son of Zechariah, in the wilderness, and he went into all the region preaching a baptism of repentance for the forgiveness of sins, so John receives the word of God as a prophet does, and, in fact, notice in Chapter 3, Verses 10-14, that Luke gives John a prophetic announcement, not simply of the one who's going to follow after him, as in Matthew and in Mark, but he teaches the people; he proclaims good news concerning the use of possessions, which is one of Luke's major themes. The way you respond to God is shown by the way you use your material possessions.

The multitudes asked him "What then shall we do?" and he answered them "Let the one who has two coats share with him who has none. Let the one who has food do likewise." Tax collectors said, "What should we do?" and he says, "Collect no more than is appointed to you." Soldiers asked, "What shall we do?" and he said, "Rob no one by violence or by false accusation and be content with your wages"—in other words, don't gouge people or extort people. For Luke, the response to God's prophet is measured by the way in which one uses one's possessions, so the rich will be sent away empty, the poor will be lifted up, and this has a moral demand of participation and care for those who are poor.

Now Jesus is baptized, but notice how Luke does this. He almost removes John from the scene. This is 3:21, "Now when all the people were baptized and when Jesus also had been baptized," and while he was praying he uses three clauses in Greek to shift John from the scene so that we see this as a response to Jesus's prayer, that heaven was opened, the Holy Spirit descended upon him in bodily form as a dove, and a voice came from heaven, "Thou art my beloved son; with thee I am well pleased."

Luke follows this announcement from God with the genealogy. He doesn't put it at the beginning, as Matthew does, and the genealogy, notice, begins with Jesus and goes in reverse order. Jesus, when he began his ministry, was about 30 years of age, being the son, as it was supposed, of Joseph, and then the son of Heli, the son of Matthat, and so forth, and he goes all the way back, not to Abraham, but all the way back to Seth, the son of Adam, the son of God, so Luke has really emphasized Jesus's identity as the prophetic son of God, who is son of God because he is full of the Holy Spirit.

Then notice how Luke makes the same emphasis with Jesus's temptation and first preaching in the synagogue in Nazareth. In Chapter 4, Verse 1, in Mark, you will remember, right after the baptism, the spirit casts Jesus into the wilderness, almost like he was exorcising them. In Matthew, the spirit guides Jesus into the wilderness, but what does Luke say? "Jesus, full of the Holy Spirit, returned from the Jordan and was led by the spirit," and so the testing is one which is the prophet's testing in the wilderness, whether or not Jesus as prophet is going to be faithful. And then in Verse 14, Jesus returned in the power of the spirit into Galilee, and he begins preaching, so the baptism, Holy Spirit, bodily, you are the son. The genealogy says you are the son. The Holy Spirit leads him. The tester says, "Are you the son?" Jesus says. "I really am. I'm obedient to God," and the spirit leads him back into his hometown of Nazareth.

Here we have one of the most dramatic scenes in Luke's Gospel, Jesus's opening sermon in his hometown in Nazareth. This is found only in Luke. In Mark's Gospel and in Matthew's Gospel, the parallel account of Jesus's rejection by his townspeople is a very bare account, and it's found in Mark, Chapter 6, and in Matthew, Chapter 13, well after Jesus had begun doing his works. Luke moves that story to the very beginning, and he amplifies it by providing a speech by Jesus. Jesus reads from the prophet Isaiah: "The spirit of the Lord is upon me because he has anointed me." Yes, we have learned that; Luke has shown us the Holy Spirit is abundantly upon Jesus, so he is Messiah because he's anointed with the Holy Spirit. But there's more; "to preach good news to the poor. He has sent me to proclaim release to captives, sight to the blind, liberty to the oppressed, to proclaim an acceptable year of the Lord." So Luke uses this incident to show the fulfillment of the prophecy of Isaiah about an anointed one who is going to proclaim good news to the poor. Jesus is that messiah.

The immediate response from the townspeople is very positive, "What gracious words proceed from his mouth." But then Luke shows an odd thing. He says, "You're going to say to me 'why don't you do the wonders here that you're doing elsewhere'" and he says "A prophet is not acceptable in his own country," and then he proceeds virtually to taunt them by saying, "There were many widows back in Israel at the time of Elijah the prophet, but Elijah didn't help any of those widows. He helped the widow of Zarephath, the Gentile widow. There were many lepers in Israel in the time of Elisha the prophet, but Elisha didn't help any of them. He helped the Syrian general and cured him of leprosy." When his townspeople hear that, they are enraged and seek to kill Jesus.

Luke has used this moment to identify Jesus as the prophetic messiah who has a message of reversal, good news to the poor, and by implication a good news that's going to extend beyond Israel into the Gentile world. And precisely that creates a rejection of the prophet because they want the good news to be for Israel as it had been intended to be. So here we have Luke's announcement of who Jesus is and what his program is, liberation, good news to the poor, recovering of sight to the blind, liberty to the oppressed.

The next time Jesus opens this mouth in public is in Chapter 6 Verse 20. After appointing the Twelve, he comes down with them and stands on a level place with a great crowd of his disciples, and people are being healed of their diseases; and he lifts up his eyes on his disciples, and says: "Blessed are you poor, for yours is the kingdom of God. Blessed are you that are hungry, for you shall be satisfied.

Blessed are you that weep now, for you shall laugh. Blessed are you when men hate you, and exclude you; rejoice because their fathers did that to the prophets." Notice the difference for Matthew. Matthew has Jesus on the mountain. He says, Blessed are you who are poor in spirit. Blessed are you who are meek." For Luke, it is actual categories of people, the poor, those who are mourning, those who are hungry.

Furthermore, these beatitudes, these blessings, are accompanied by Luke with woes. "Woe to you who are rich, for you have your consolation now." Remember Simeon was looking for the consolation of Israel. The rich already have their consolation in their riches. "Woe to you who are full now, for you shall hunger. Woe to you that laugh now, for you shall mourn and weep. Woe to you, when everybody speaks well of you, because that's what people did of the false prophets," so acceptance and rejection is the measure of a false or true prophet. If people are accepting you, you can't be a true prophet; if they're rejecting you, you're a true prophet. Why? Because you're challenging the conventions of the world. You are saying that consolation is not a matter of being wealthy but a matter of being poor. This is a reversal of human expectations.

Notice also in Luke 7:22, when John the Baptist sends messengers to Jesus asking, "Are you the one that we're looking for?" Jesus says, "Go, and tell John what you have seen and heard: the blind receive their sight, the lame walk, lepers are cleansed, the deaf hear, the dead are raised up, and the poor have good news preached to them. And blessed is he who does not offense at me." He goes on to identify John as a prophet and as more than a prophet, so the proclamation of the good news to the poor is the sign or the symbol of everything that Jesus is doing—raising the dead, giving sight to the blind and so forth—so that Luke's language about possessions has two levels.

At one level, it has a symbolic valence; it represents those who are the outcast and the marginalized of society for whatever reason, who's called to be in God's favor. That might be called a symbolic valence. At another level, he intends the response to that call must be enacted by the use of possessions. How do you use your possessions? We saw that already signaled in John the Baptist;

namely, do you share your possessions with others? So this is going to be something more public then the ministry of Jesus in Mark and in Matthew. Luke portrays Jesus's ministry as a prophetic call to inclusion in God's people. Luke's Jesus is more political in the obvious sense of that word than the Jesus of Mark and Matthew.

Jesus's healing of the sick both fulfills the prophetic statements about this, but it touches those who through demonic possession or illness or sin are separated from God's people, or stigmatized, so, again, when Luke talks about Jesus calling sinners and a physician is needed by those who are sick, not the well, and his followers are identified as sinners, being a sinner stands on the same plane as those who are filled with unclean spirits, or those who have fever or leprosy or are paralyzed or are women or are children; namely, they are all those who are excluded from full participation in the ritual, the cultic, the political life of the nation, and so Jesus's ministry is remarkable in Luke's Gospel for the way in which Jesus reaches out and touches all those who were stigmatized and separated, so that physical and spiritual healing are at the same time a kind of salvation that is social in character.

Luke's language is deliberately ambiguous here. The term *sozein* in Greek means to heal but also means to save, and so when Jesus says to somebody, "Your faith has saved you," it means at one level your faith has healed you but also faith is the response by which one becomes part of this restored people that is gathering around the prophet, so your faith also saves you. Notice that in Luke's Gospel virtually all of the healings ensue in the return of the healed person to society so that the end point of healing is being part of a people. It is a social reality and not simply a personal reality. It is not spiritual in the sense that now you're headed straight; it's rather that you've been brought within this people.

Luke uses table fellowship also as a way of symbolizing Jesus's program of healing the people; thus, he is eating with tax collectors and sinners when he's challenged in Chapter 5, "Why are you doing this?" and he says, "It is the sick people who need a physician. I have come not to call the righteous, but to call the sinners," so sickness and sin are on a continuum in Luke. It's when Jesus is eating with tax collectors and sinners that the Pharisees attack him in Chapter 7, Verse 34, and call him somebody who associates with sinners, and to demonstrate in fact that that's the case, Luke tells the story only in Luke Chapter 7, Verses 36-52, of the woman, the sinner in the city, who comes and anoints Jesus's feet with her tears and dries them with her hair, and Jesus tells her that she is acceptable because of her repentance, in contrast to his host, a Pharisee, who is a righteous person but does not receive Jesus hospitably.

So we now get another division. In the narrative itself of Luke, sinners and the outcast and the poor are the new righteous, whereas those who are powerful and righteous are those who are being excluded, and so the Pharisees stand as the model of those who are being excluded from the people, so Luke's distinctive parables also serve to interpret this prophetic ministry of healing and restoration. The parable of the Good Samaritan in Chapter 10, Verses 29-37, the unexpected help from an outsider—it's a Jewish man who is injured—it's a despised Samaritan who shows himself to be a neighbor to this person. But, above all, the story of the prodigal son in Chapter 15, Verses 11-32, which actually is an extension of two other parables of the lost sheep, and the man leaves 99 sheep and goes and finds that one and brings him back, or the woman who loses a coin, and she sweeps and sweeps and sweeps until she finds one coin, and then the story of the son, the lost son, and the father who brings him back.

But that story climaxes with the elder son who resents the mercy shown to the younger son and refuses to come in and share at the party because he's always kept the rules and now the father has no discrimination, he throws the door open to his profligate son and welcomes him home. Notice the way in which Luke introduces those three parables of the lost and found. In Chapter 15:1-2, "Now the tax collectors and sinners were all drawing near to hear him. And the Pharisees and the scribes murmured, saying, 'This man receives sinners and eats with them.'" The scribes and the Pharisees represent the older son; they've always kept the rules. They resent Jesus's ministry of inclusion of others.

Finally, in Luke's Gospel, Jesus is himself a charismatic figure whose radical matter of life exemplifies his program. He's led by the spirit; he's obedient to God. Luke shows Jesus constantly in prayer, in his baptism before he chooses the Twelve, at the transfiguration. He is praying in Chapter 11, when he teaches the disciples the Lord's Prayer. In the garden at his death, Jesus is poor and a wanderer who depends upon the hospitality of others, and Jesus exercises a form of leadership that's based on service of others. Look particularly at the sayings of Jesus at the Last Supper in Chapter 22, Verses 24-27, where Jesus says that among the Gentiles leaders rule and dominate others but it should not be that way among you. Your leadership should be a matter of service, and then he says, "I am among you as one who serves."

So Jesus gives a servant leadership within the people, and finally he calls his followers to a radical discipleship that imitates the prophetic life of Jesus, most strikingly in Chapter 14, where Jesus says, "If anyone comes to me and does not hate his own father and mother and wife and children and brothers and sisters, yes, even his own life, he cannot be my disciple," and then in Verse 32, "Whoever of you does not renounce all that he has cannot be my disciple."

Lecture Nineteen
Gospel of Luke—The Prophet and the People

Scope:

The prophet visits God's people in order to gather them into a restored people. The prophet's call demands conversion, a real change of life. Those who respond to the prophet's radical demands with faith find a place at his table. Those who reject his demands find themselves displaced from their place in the people. In Luke's Gospel, Jesus's last journey to Jerusalem is an extended one, in which he forms a people around himself and instructs them. Luke's passion account, in turn, is distinctive both for its portrayal of Jesus and for the way in which blame for Jesus's death is shifted toward Jewish leaders and away from the ordinary Jewish people.

Outline

I.   The suggestion that Luke-Acts is best understood as a Hellenistic biography has merit but omits the two most important characters.

   A. Unquestionably, aspects of Luke-Acts resemble biographies of philosophers and their students.

       1. The portrayal of Jesus as prophet overlaps the stereotype of the Cynic philosopher.

       2. The apostles in Acts are shaded to resemble philosophers in their courage before tyrants.

   B. But Luke-Acts is better understood as history because it opens up the story of Jesus and his followers to a much larger stage.

       1. In Mark, there is an almost claustrophobic focus on Jesus and the disciples.

       2. In Matthew, the story is opened up to conflict with formative Judaism.

       3. Luke connects the story to larger world history and, above all, to the biblical story.

   C. Luke's main characters are the God of Israel (whose son Jesus is) and the people of Israel (whom the prophet Jesus calls to repentance), and the main crisis is whether God has been truly faithful to the people and whether the people will prove faithful to God.

II. The prophet Jesus embodies God's "visitation" of the people for their "salvation."

   A. The canticles of the infancy narrative place John and Jesus in the frame of God's intervention in history on the side of Israel (1:46–55; 1:68–80).

   B. Jesus not only announces "good news to the poor" and the outcast, but he demands, as did John, a repentance that shows itself in a change of life.

   1. The positive response to the prophet is a "faith" that means joining his radical social program.

   2. Repentance means changing patterns of life in accordance with the prophet's program, especially in the use of material possessions.

   C. If the "poor" stand symbolically for those who respond in faith, the "rich" play the narrative role of the powerful and privileged who "have no need of comfort" and fail to repent (6:24–26; 16:14; 18:18–23).

   D. The response of Zacchaeus, the chief tax-gatherer, expresses the theme of salvation and repentance crisply (19:1–10).

III. Luke portrays Jesus's long journey to Jerusalem as a prophetic progression that forms a people.

   A. Luke inserts the bulk of his Q and L material into this constructed journey: Jesus is constantly said to be on the way to the city "with his disciples."

   1. As he moves toward the city, he announces his death in a series of predictions.

   2. He works few wonders but mostly teaches in several settings, especially on the road and while at table.

   B. Luke carefully rotates Jesus's speech among three groups: the crowd, the opponents, and the disciples. To each group, Jesus speaks appropriately.

1. To the crowd, he issues warnings and calls to repent before it is too late.
2. To enemies (the Pharisees and lawyers) he tells parables of rejection (14:15–24).
3. To the disciples called from the crowd, he provides instruction on prayer (11:1), the use of possessions, and perseverance (12:22–34).

C. Luke shows that the small group of the journey's start (8:1–3) turns into a "great crowd of disciples" (19:37) that greets him as he enters the city as "the king who comes in the name of the Lord."

IV. Luke's passion account follows the same storyline as in Matthew and Mark but with a distinct emphasis.

A. Jesus is presented in philosophical/prophet terms as a figure who is in control of his feelings, exercises authority to the end, and dies with a prayer of acceptance on his lips. In contrast to Mark and Matthew, where Jesus is recognized by his executioner as the "son of God," in Luke, Jesus is recognized by his executioner as "a righteous man."(23:47).

B. The ordinary people of the city—who thronged to Jesus as a teacher (21:38)—play little role in the plot against him. In contrast to Matthew, who puts the blame on the whole populace, in Luke's Gospel, it is the leadership that works against Jesus. At his death, the populace repents (23:48–49).

Essential Reading:
The Gospel of Luke, 9–23.

Supplementary Reading:
D. P. Moessner, *Lord of the Banquet: The Literary and Theological Significance of the Lukan Travel Narrative* (Minneapolis: Fortress Press, 1989).

J. H. Neyrey, *The Passion According to Luke: A Redactional Study of Luke's Soteriology* (New York: Paulist Press, 1985).

Questions to Consider:

1. Discuss the way in which Luke has a more "political" understanding of the "kingdom of God."

2. What is the effect of Luke's distinctive portrayal of Jesus and the people of Israel in his passion narrative?

Lecture Nineteen—Transcript
Gospel of Luke—The Prophet and the People

In the previous lecture, I suggested that Luke's Gospel portrays Jesus as a prophet who brings God's visitation to the people of Israel in order to restore it to its authentic identity, calling it to a vision of human life that includes all those who had been marginalized by poverty, stigma, sickness, sin, into full fellowship. The prophet himself witnesses to God by a life totally dedicated to God, a life of poverty, of prayer, of service to others, led by the Holy Spirit, and this prophet calls his disciples into the same radical lifestyle. In this presentation, I want to pursue further this theme of the prophet and the people, with the emphasis on the prophet's relationship to the people.

The suggestion that Luke-Acts is best understood as a Hellenistic biography does have some merit, but it omits the two most important characters in the story. There are undoubtedly aspects of Luke-Acts that resemble biographies of philosophers and their students, such as were written by Diogenes Laertius and Iamblichus, *The Lives of Eminent Philosophers* by Diogenes Laertius, and Iamblichus's *Life of Pythagoras*. The portrayal of Jesus as prophet overlaps the stereotype of the Cynic philosopher so that Jesus as prophet looks very much like Jesus as Cynic philosopher. The Cynic philosopher goes about dressed in a robe and sandals and a staff and practices poverty and exercises boldness in confronting others, and that matches pretty well the image of Jesus in Luke's Gospel.

Even more so, the apostles in Acts are shaded to resemble philosophers in their courage before tyrants. In the Acts of the Apostles, Chapter 4, when Peter and John are called before the Sanhedrin, one of my favorite passages is when Peter confronts the leaders with a tremendous boldness. The author notes in 4:13, "Now when they saw the boldness"—and the word here is *parrhesia*, which in Greek was used specifically for the boldness of philosophers and the frankness of philosophers in the face of tyranny—"when they saw the boldness of Peter and John and perceived that they were uneducated, common men, they wondered (and here's my favored part), and they recognized that they had been with Jesus." In other words, there is a link between the boldness of the apostles and the boldness that we find in Jesus.

Just a little bit later on in 4:19, Peter says "Whether it is right in the sight of God to listen to you rather than to God, you must judge." This is a clear allusion to Socrates when called to trial, that one must obey God rather than humans, so there is this portrayal of the apostles in philosophical terms. Notice Luke puts Paul before the Epicurean and Stoic philosophers in the city of Athens in his great Areopagus speech and has Paul speak as though he were a philosopher. The whole last portion of Acts is devoted to Paul's defense speeches that he makes before various kings and tyrants.

We see at the end of Chapter 26, Paul says, "King Agrippa, do you believe the prophets? I know that you believe." And Agrippa said to Paul, "In a short time I think you will make me a Christian," or as I prefer to translate it, you're trying to get me to play the Christian a little bit, and Paul says, "Whether short or long, I would to God that not only you but also all who hear me this day might become such as I am, except for these chains." Paul is a perfect philosopher challenging the rulers of the world.

But despite these biographical notes, Luke/Acts is better understood as history because it opens up the story of Jesus and his followers to a much larger stage. We saw in Mark there was an almost claustrophobic focus on Jesus and the disciples, the drama of discipleship. In Matthew, we saw that the story of Jesus and the disciples opened up a bit to formative Judaism, what I call "the synagogue down the street." But Luke deliberately places the story of Jesus and his followers into a larger world history and above all to the Biblical story, so this is why Luke at every point in the story notes who were the local rulers, who was in charge of things. This is a way of showing, as Paul says before Agrippa in Chapter 26, Verse 26, of Acts, "These things did not happen in the corner." In other words, they are public; they are part of world history and not simply a sectarian history.

But as I said, the notion of biography is too small because it leaves out the two characters who are most important. One character is that of God, the God of Israel, whose son Jesus is. This character of God is not visible in the story, but is everywhere operative. It is God who makes things happen in the story, and it is the same God who was at work in the story of Israel. The second character is the people of Israel itself who God chose long ago, who shaped as God's people through covenant and who sends them the prophet to call them to repentance, so the main crisis in Luke-Acts is whether God has truly been faithful to this people and whether the people will prove faithful to God. This is the real drama, the drama of the prophet and the people.

That is why Luke uses geography and prophecy in order to fix the reader's attention on that middle Jerusalem part of his story between Luke 19 and Acts 8 because that is where the pivotal events take place. After Acts 8, it's simply denouement; the major crisis in the story has been resolved. Let's begin over this lecture and the next lecture to begin to fill in the story of the people. The prophet Jesus then embodies God's visitation of the people. That word visitation sounds archaic, but it comes from the Biblical language of God's intervention for the people, God's coming among the people as in the story of the exodus, and Luke uses that archaic language deliberately for what Jesus is doing. God wants to call his people to salvation, which is to be restored. Notice that Zechariah, the father of John the Baptist, when he is filled with the Holy Spirit in Chapter 1, Verse 67, he prophesied, as Luke says, saying:

68: "Blessed be the Lord God of Israel, for he has visited and redeemed his people,

69: he has raised up a horn of salvation for us in the house of his servant David,

70: as he spoke by the holy prophets from of old,

71: that we should be saved from our enemies,

72: so that he would remember his holy covenant,

73: the oath he swore to our father Abraham,

©2004 The Teaching Company Limited Partnership

74: to grant us that we, being delivered from the hand of our enemies, might serve him without fear,

75: in holiness and righteousness before him all the days of our life.

Zechariah is here prophesying completely within the framework of pious Israel. God's visitation is meant for his people in fulfillment of his covenant with Abraham in memory of his servant David.

In the Gospel, this is how the story is focused. Jesus announces not only good news to the poor and the outcast, he demands, as did his forerunner and his cousin John, of repentance, the works of righteousness that show themselves in a change of light. This *metanoia*, this conversion, is not simply changing one's mind; it is changing one's behavior—it is a political response—so the positive response to the prophet Jesus and the gospel is this faith, not a faith that he is divine, rather, an acceptance of his program. It is a willingness to get, if you will, on the same page as the prophet's vision of how humans should be by joining his radical social program, recognizing that he is the prophet, allowing him to restore the outcasts to the people. Repentance means changing patterns of life in accord with the prophet's program, as I mentioned, above all with respect to the use of material possessions, and so Jesus tells them "Fear not, little flock, for it is your father's good pleasure to give you the kingdom."

They don't have to fear; they have what is most essential, namely, a place in God's kingdom. Therefore, sell your possessions, give alms, provide yourself with purses that do not grow old with a treasure in the heavens that does not fail, where no thief approaches, no moth destroys, for where your treasure is, there will your heart be also. This is Chapter 12, Verses 32-34, which follows upon an even longer discourse about not having anxiety about how you clothe yourself or how you feed yourself. It's not only don't be anxious, but you should sell your possessions and give alms, so just as with John the Baptist, so with Jesus, the proper response to the prophet is to divest oneself of power, to divest oneself a possession, not simply as a divestment but to give alms and to strengthen others so that there is this other directedness to the formation of a prophetic people.

If, in the Gospel, the poor, as I have suggested, stand symbolically for those who respond in faith and therefore are comforted by this gift of the prophet, the rich play the narrative role of the powerful and the privileged, who, as 6:24, says have no need of comfort or have their comfort already and who fail to repent. Within the narrative then, if the poor can also be the sick and the sinners, so the rich are the Pharisees and the chief priests and the powerful. In other words, they are the people who are at the very center of the establishment, the very center of the cultic and ritual life of Israel. They are the powerful ones who are going to be put down from their thrones as the poor are lifted up by the work of God. There is this reversal, you see.

A lovely story of Zacchaeus, the chief tax collector, expresses the theme of salvation and repentance with marvelous crispness. As he entered Jericho (this is a story found only in Luke), as he entered Jericho and was passing through, there was a man named Zacchaeus. He was a chief tax collector and rich. Notice that he combines oxymoronically two opposite qualities. As a rich man, he ought to be among the outcast; as a tax collector, he's among the sinners. Which way is Zacchaeus going to tilt? He sought to see who Jesus was, but because he was small of stature he could not see him on account of the crowd, so he ran on ahead, climbed up into a sycamore tree (the stuff of Sunday school lessons from the beginning of time) to see Jesus, for he was to pass that way.

Jesus came. He looked up. "Zacchaeus, make haste, come down. I must stay at your house today." He made haste, came down, received him joyfully. Here's the older brother again. When they saw it, they all murmured and said, "He's gone in to be the guest of a man who was a sinner," and Zacchaeus stood and said to the Lord, "Behold Lord, the half of my goods I give to the poor, and if I have defrauded anyone of anything I restore it fourfold." Zacchaeus is rich; he ought to be on the outside, but he repents by divesting himself of his possessions, by restoring to the poor what he took from them fourfold.

Therefore, Jesus says, "Today salvation has come to this house since he also is a son of Abraham," so being a son of Abraham is to respond appropriately to the prophet's program of sharing possessions and of helping the poor. He says "For the Son of man came to seek and to save what was lost," an echo obviously of those three parables of the lost sheep, the lost coin, and the lost son in Chapter 15 that we referred to in the previous lecture. So this is how we are to read Luke's plot. The good news to the poor is a call to join the people. The rich are those who resist and who fail to join this restored people.

Let's look at the central portion of Luke's narrative, Chapter 9-19, this long journey following Peter's confession, the transfiguration account. Jesus points his face toward Jerusalem and heads toward his death as a prophetic progression that also in Luke's account helps to form the people around the prophet. As I mentioned earlier, Luke inserts the bulk of his Q and L material into this journey, which he himself has constructed. He reminds us some 17 times that he's on his way, he's on his way to Jerusalem, and he goes there with his disciples. This is where Luke uses the term *mathetes* or *mathete*, disciple, disciples, more often than any other place in his narrative.

As the prophet moves towards the city, he repeatedly announces his death, so he is predicting his death; so we know, as we did in Mark, that the prophet is one who is heading toward the ultimate rejection of the prophet, namely, his death. In this section of the story, Jesus works very few wonders. Mostly he teaches. This is where Jesus is talking all the time, on the road and at table, so Luke provides this image of somebody who's walking along, invited, shown hospitality, (true hospitality in the case of Martha and Mary; false hospitality when the Pharisees invite him to dinner), but the result is that we get this wonderful biographical sense of Jesus so that when somebody comes up and says, "I want to be a disciple, but first let me go bury my parents," and Jesus says, "Let the dead bury their dead," we have this sense of urgency and of movement which in Matthew that saying is found in the middle of a lecture and doesn't have the same kind of force.

As Jesus moves towards the city, Luke carefully notes how Jesus speaks to different groups and rotates Jesus's speech among these groups. There're three groups: the crowd, *ochlos*; the opponents, largely here the Pharisees and the lawyers with a few scribes and chief priests thrown in; and the disciples, the *mathete*. Luke will note that Jesus says this to this group and this to this group and that to that group in a kind of rotating fashion. To each group, Luke has Jesus say things that are appropriate to that group. To the crowd that is surrounding Jesus as he is making his way to Jerusalem, Luke has Jesus issue prophetic warnings, calls to discipleship.

"Woe to you, Cho-ra-zin! woe to you, Beth-sa-i-da!" This sounds like a prophet, doesn't it? "If the mighty works done in you had been done in Tyre and Sidon, they would have repented long ago, sitting in sackcloth and ashes. But it shall be more tolerable in the judgment for Tyre and Sidon than for you. And you, Caper'na-um, will you be exalted to heaven? You shall be brought down to Hades." This is the prophet warning, challenging, calling people to repent before it's too late. Enter through the narrow gate, he says; people will come from east and west and will sit at the table, but you won't have a chance to be there.

To the enemies who confront him on the road, Jesus tells parables that have a note of rejection to them. In Chapter 14, Verses 15- 24, we have Jesus already at the table on the Sabbath invited by a ruler who belonged to the Pharisees, another twofer—he's a Pharisee and he's a ruler. We know he's not going to be a good guy in the narrative. Sure enough, somebody with a disease comes into the room, Jesus heals him, and the Pharisees object. Then Jesus tells them a parable about people who are invited to a banquet. They shouldn't seek the first places but the last places so they can be brought higher because, he says, the person who humbles himself will be exalted and the person who exalts himself will be humbled, obviously a lesson to these rulers and Pharisees who, according to the custom in antiquity, occupied the best places at table.

But then he says to the man who had invited him, "When you give a dinner or a banquet, do not invite your friends or your brothers or your kinsmen or your rich neighbors, lest they invite you in return, and you be repaid"—the old law of give so that you get in return. "But when you give a feast, invite the poor, the maimed, the lame, the blind, and you will be blessed, because they cannot repay you. You will be blessed in the resurrection of the dead." Then somebody says, "Blessed are those who shall eat bread in the kingdom of God!" this happy pious thought when he hears the word, the kingdom of God, but then Jesus tells the parable of the great banquet in which a man invites people and they fail to come.

Why? "Because I bought a field, and I must go out and see it." "I bought five yoke of oxen, and I have to take care of them." "I've married a wife and therefore I cannot come," and so Jesus says the man sends them out to the hedgerows and goes and gets all the winos, gets all the people, the homeless, and brings them in, the people of the lanes of the city, the poor, the maimed, the blind, and the lame because, he says, "I tell you, none of those men who were first invited shall taste my banquet." We have here a complex set of teachings, but clearly the Pharisees who do not show Jesus appropriate hospitality are being taught, are being warned about the way in which they behave and they had better watch out because they're not going to be part of the banquet if they stay rich, involved with their oxen, involved with their families, involved with the fields that they have bought.

That's to the crowd warnings and calls to discipleship, to the opponents again warnings that they are being left out, but to the people from the crowd who become disciples, on this journey Jesus gives the bulk of his positive teaching on discipleship. First, on prayer, Jesus is in prayer in Chapter 11, Verse 1: "He was praying in a certain place, and when he ceased, one of his disciples said to him, 'Lord, teach us to pray, as John taught his disciples,'" and so Jesus here—remember, Matthew taught the Lord's Prayer in the Sermon on the Mount—here Jesus says, "When you pray, say: 'Father, hallowed be thy name. Thy kingdom come. Give us each day our daily bread; and forgive us our sins, for we ourselves forgive every one who is indebted to us; and lead us not into temptation,'" a much shorter version of the Lord's Prayer in Luke.

He also teaches them on the use of possessions. As we saw in Chapter 12, Verses 22-34, we have this long teaching on not being anxious, about what you shall eat, or your life, or what you should put on your body, "for life is more than food and the body more than clothing," and then he goes on to say that they should sell their positions and give alms to others. Finally, he teaches them as well on the need to have perseverance, this marvelous story of the widow and the unjust judge. He taught them a parable to the effect that they ought always to pray and not lose heart.

2: He said, "In a certain city there was a judge who feared neither God nor humans;

3: and there was a widow in that city who kept coming to him and saying, `Vindicate me against my adversary.'

4: For a while he refused; but afterward he said to himself, `Though I neither fear God nor regard man,

5: yet because this widow bothers me, I shall vindicate her, or she will wear me out by her continual coming.'"

Actually, the Greek phrase there can be translated, "She will give me a black eye by her continual coming," either physically or by reputation.

6: And the Lord said, "Hear what the unrighteous judge says.

7: And will not God vindicate his elect, who cry out to him day and night? Will he delay long over them?

8: I tell you, he will vindicate them speedily. Nevertheless, when the Son of man comes, will he find faith on earth?"

So this is a teaching on perseverance and stick-to-itiveness in prayer, so prayer, possessions, perseverance, positive teaching to his disciples on the road, so here's what Luke has done in this journey. He has the prophet moving towards his death, predicting it, and as he is going, calling out warnings to the people, rejecting his opponents who do not accept him as a prophet. Notice in Chapter 16, after Jesus teaches that you cannot have both God and Mammon as your master, Luke says, "And the Pharisees who were lovers of money made fun of him," and so his opponents are rejecting him, and those who accept him he gives positive teachings.

Notice that in this journey, Luke has accomplished another effect. Right before the journey begins in Chapter 8, Verses 1-3, Luke names Jesus's community. It was the Twelve and it was a handful of women who were supporting him. By the time he reaches the city in Chapter 19, Verse 37, Luke says there was a great *plethos*, a great mob of disciples who greeted Jesus as king, who come in the name of the Lord, so, in effect, he has created a restored people around the prophet, and then when Jesus enters into the city, Jesus occupies the temple and teaches there and the people come to him gladly.

This leads us to Luke's passion account, which again has distinctive characteristics. Like Matthew, he follows Mark's basic passion account; this is the place, as I've mentioned repeatedly, where the Gospels are most in agreement, but Luke deviates from Mark in some important ways. First, Jesus is presented in philosophical prophetic terms as a man who is much more in control of his feelings. Notice at the Last Supper, Jesus engages in what might almost be called a Socratic farewell discourse, teaching his disciples about the proper mode of servant leadership among them. In the garden, it is his disciples who are filled with fear, not Jesus. Jesus enters into an agony, which means in Greek a struggle, which is like a wrestler engaging what he has to face and coming through it in obedience, but he's not a fearful figure; he is a powerful philosophical figure.

He exercises his authority to the end. He prophesies to the daughters of Jerusalem who weep over him and warns them about what is going to happen. He tells the thief who is executed with him that this day you will be with me in paradise. He exemplifies the attitude of the righteous person by saying, "Father, forgive them for they do not know what they do." This is not found in Mark or Matthew. Jesus has the capacity to forgive even his executioners. Most notably, notice that at the moment of death, where in Matthew and in Mark Jesus cries out, "My God, my God, why have you forsaken me?" which is the first verse of Psalm 22, in Luke, Jesus hands over his spirit and says, "Father, into your hands I commend my spirit." This is a quotation from another Psalm, Psalm 31, Verse 5, which in Judaism is the recommended Psalm with which a righteous man should die. The centurion who in Mark and Matthew called Jesus God's son, here the centurion said, "This truly is a righteous man." The portrayal of Jesus is very different, downplaying the physical suffering, downplaying the emotional agony, portraying Jesus as a righteous man, prophetic figure to the end.

The other aspect of this, and here again, particularly because of the way in which people do things with Gospels—this should be emphasized—in contrast to Matthew, who deliberately brings down the blood guilt on the Jewish population as a whole and on their children, Luke makes every effort to put the blame only on the leaders of the people. He removes, in scene after scene, he removes the ordinary populace from participation in these events. Notice that at the death of Jesus it is the leaders of the people who pass by the cross mocking him. Luke says that the populace, which had come to the execution as to a spectacle, observers, when they saw what had happened, returned to the city beating their breasts, which is a gesture of repentance. At the end, in other words, Luke has shown us a people that is ready to get with the prophet's program in the Acts of the Apostles.

Lecture Twenty
Acts of the Apostles—The Prophet's Movement

Scope:

In the Acts of the Apostles, Jesus's followers prove themselves to be prophetic successors. Like Moses and like Jesus, they are filled with the Holy Spirit, speak God's word boldly, and work signs and wonders. They exemplify the radical lifestyle in the community of possessions. They witness boldly before courts and kings. And they extend Jesus's understanding of God's people by an even more radical inclusion than that of Jesus himself, when the Gentiles are accepted into the people without circumcision and the obligation to observe the Law.

Outline

I. Reading Acts as the continuation of Luke's Gospel reveals a distinctive understanding of history.

    A. At the surface level, it is a straightforward account of the events of Christianity's first great expansion from Jerusalem to Rome.

        1. Jesus's programmatic prophecy in Acts 1:8 provides a table of contents: Jerusalem (1–8); Judaea and Samaria (8–12); to the ends of the world, that is, Rome (13–28).

        2. It is a selective account, with particular attention given to Peter and Paul and the transmission of the good news from Jews to Gentiles.

    B. At a deeper level, Acts portrays the church as the continuation of the prophetic movement started by Jesus.

        1. The bestowal of the Holy Spirit on the disciples means that they are empowered as Jesus was.

        2. All the protagonists are described in stereotypical prophetic terms as they proclaim the "good news" about what God had done in Jesus.

        3. Thus, Luke's portrayal of the disciples is not as negative as it is in Mark.

II. The first church in Jerusalem is portrayed as the restoration of Israel for which Jesus worked.

  A. The outpouring of the Holy Spirit on all flesh is interpreted as the sign of the resurrection and exaltation of Jesus (2:1–37).

  B. Those who "save themselves from this evil generation" fulfill the prophetic program.

  1. They share their possessions fully so that no one was in need (2:41–47; 4:32–37).

  2. The apostles continue to heal as a "sign of salvation" of the people (3:1–26).

  C. The thousands of Jews who join the community demonstrate Luke's two major concerns.

  1. Even though his people—or, mainly, their leaders—rejected God's first "visitation," he remained faithful and provided another chance for repentance through the preaching of the apostles.

  2. Even though they had rejected Jesus, many of the Jews accepted "the prophet whom God raised up," with the result that they became the authentic remnant of Israel.

  3. The theological point that Luke is making here is that the mission to the Gentiles, especially as carried on by Paul, is not a replacement of Israel but a continuation.

III. The apostles are portrayed as prophets who continue Jesus's radical manner of life in new circumstances.

  A. They share their possessions and manifest "servant leadership" by their "waiting at tables" (4:32–37; 6:1–7).

  B. They pray at every moment of crisis, just as Jesus had done, and are empowered by the Holy Spirit, as he was (4:23–31).

  C. They heal the outcast of the people, breaking the boundaries of separation and stigma caused by illness (5:12–16; 6:4–8; 8:32–43).

  D. They bear witness boldly, even in the face of trial, persecution, and death (4:5–22; 5:17–42; 6:8–7:60; 22:1–21; 23:1–11; 24:10–21; 26:2–23).

IV. The church continues the radical prophetic program of table-fellowship for the outcast through the bold initiative of including Gentiles without requiring circumcision and the observance of Torah.

    A. As part of their doctrine of separateness, Jews did not eat with Gentiles. Thus, the church was radical in its program of table-fellowship that included Gentiles.

    B. Luke tells the story as one of God's initiative and human discernment, debate, and decision-making (Acts 10–15).

    C. Luke suggests that the church was even more radical in its vision than Jesus was: Accepting Gentiles without circumcision and Law meant accepting God's new work more than the precedent of scripture.

Essential Reading:

The Acts of the Apostles.

Supplementary Reading:

L. T. Johnson, *The Literary Function of Possessions in Luke-Acts* (SBLDS 39; Missoula: Scholars Press, 1977).

S. Garrett, *The Demise of the Devil: Magic and the Demonic in Luke's Writings* (Minneapolis: Fortress Press, 1989).

Questions to Consider:

1. Comment on this proposition: "Luke's account of the Jerusalem church shows that God has proven faithful to Israel."

2. Why can the acceptance of Gentile believers without requiring circumcision and the observance of the Law be regarded as a radical realization of the prophetic vision of Luke's Jesus?

Lecture Twenty—Transcript
Acts of the Apostles—The Prophet's Movement

Since the New Testament writings were first put into their canonical form, the Gospel of Luke and the Acts of the Apostles have been separated. We don't know when this took place. We have no manuscripts in which they appear as a single literary composition, so Luke was quickly grouped with Matthew and Mark and John as one of the Gospels, more recently as a Synoptic Gospel that could be read in parallel columns with Matthew and Mark, while Acts has tended to be read as a straightforward history of early Christianity that happens to introduce the character of Paul, so we have the Four Gospels, [Matthew, Mark], Luke, John, then the Acts of the Apostles, and then Paul's letters in the ordinary canonical arrangement.

The effect of this canonical arrangement is to disable us from really seeing how Luke and Acts are a single literary enterprise. But our task in this course is to read the Gospels as literary compositions, and as a literary composition there is no doubt that Luke's good news includes both the story of Jesus and the story of the church or, perhaps better, the story of Jesus as it continues in the story of the church. So it's appropriate in a course on Jesus and the Gospels to devote at least one session to the continuation of Luke's Gospel in the Acts of the Apostles, considered as the prophets' movement.

Reading Acts as the continuation of Luke's Gospel reveals a distinctive understanding of history. At the surface level, Acts appears to be a straightforward account of the events of Christianity's first-grade expansion from Jerusalem to Rome. You will recall that in a very early lecture in this course, I talked about Acts as providing the narrative framework for Christianity's first expansion and how it was limited in what it told us but nevertheless essential in providing a kind of geographic and chronological framework for Christianity's first movement, so it does that job well. Jesus's programmatic prophecy in Acts 1:8 provides a kind of table of contents in which the good news reaches from Jerusalem, in

Chapters 1-8, Judea, and Samaria, in 8-12, to the ends of the earth, which is Rome, in 13:28.

But it is, as we have seen, a selective historical account, with particular attention given to Peter and Paul and above all to the demographic transition from Jew to Gentile, how the good news reaches the Gentiles, so what Isaiah says in Luke's version of introducing John the Baptist, that all flesh shall see the salvation of God, is anticipated from the beginning. One of the great themes of Luke is how the good news reaches the Gentiles. At this level, it's a pretty straightforward history, but at a deeper level Acts portrays the church as the continuation of the prophetic movement started by Jesus.

This would be a startling statement to many of my fellow scholars, who tend to view Acts and have tended to view Acts either as a straightforward history and therefore to be judged on the basis of is it good history or bad history, on the basis of is it factual or is it fictional (although we've seen that those two terms can very well go together; you can have fact within fictional shaping); or when Acts is read as bad history and therefore theology (it's an interesting move) and read as a theological work, it has tended to be viewed as a betrayal of Jesus rather than a continuation of Jesus.

Lutheran Protestant scholars who dominated New Testament scholarship had the way of characterizing Acts as a *theologia gloriae*, a theology of glory. They emphasized the triumph of Christianity that takes place in Acts, the wonders that are worked and so forth, and they viewed this as a rejection or a betrayal of the *theologia crucis*, the theology of the cross that they associated with St. Paul, the life of service and suffering and so forth. Fascinatingly, more recent historical Jesus scholars have taken much the same approach, although not in the same terms. Virtually every historical Jesus on offer at Barnes & Noble and Borders these days—and I'm talking about left-wing as well as right-wing approaches to historical Jesus—are drawn from the Gospel of Luke. It is Luke 24/7 on the historical Jesus front.

Luke's Jesus is a Jesus that profoundly appeals to us. He's public, he's political, he's prophetic, he's challenging the conventions of society, he's calling for the reversal of norms. This is deeply appealing, but for the same historical Jesus people who find Luke's Jesus appealing, Acts is once more a betrayal. It's institutionalized; it's about the apostles. Jesus is good on women; Acts is bad on women. What's puzzling about this of course is the premise that Luke, who created the Jesus in the Gospel, should have so quickly forgotten what he had done in the Gospel in his portrayal of Acts. I suggest that maybe we need to reexamine what Luke is really saying in the Acts of the Apostles. I find it more likely that Luke wants us to see Acts as a continuation of the prophets' program than he should have forgotten what he said about Jesus when he went on to describe what he said about the apostles, and that's the approach I'm going to take in this lecture, how Acts is a continuation of the prophetic movement started by Jesus.

Let's begin with Pentecost; the bestowal of the Holy Spirit on the disciples obviously matches the prophetic bestowal of the spirit on Jesus in his baptism and his being led by the spirit. This account of the outpouring of the Holy Spirit, notice, is interpreted by Peter in Acts 2:17-21 in terms of a long citation from the prophet Joel, Chapter 2, Verses 20-32, with slight emendations, which I will note. "And in the last days it shall be, God declares, that I will pour out my Spirit upon all flesh, and your sons and your daughters shall prophesy, and your young men shall see visions, and your old men shall dream dreams; yea, and on my menservants and my maidservants in those days (my dula and my dule, in those days) I shall pour out my Spirit," and now Luke adds to this "and they shall prophesy."

Luke adds a line to Joel which emphasizes prophecy, "and I will show wonders in the heaven above," and now Luke adds this phrase, "signs on the earth beneath, blood, and fire, and vapor of smoke; the sun shall be turned into darkness and the moon into blood, before the day of the Lord comes, the great and manifest day. And it shall be that whoever calls on the name of the Lord shall be saved." What is striking about this is that this outpouring of the spirit on the Twelve and on the community of women that had followed Jesus from Galilee and on Jesus's mother, who's also in that group, as Luke describes it, we have in effect now not a prophet who is filled with the spirit but a people who is filled with the prophetic spirit.

As Peter proceeds to interpret this Holy Spirit, he interprets it in terms of the resurrection of Jesus. "This Jesus, whom you rejected, God raised up, and of that we all are witnesses; being therefore exalted at the right hand of God and having received from the father the promise of the Holy Spirit, he has poured out this which you see and hear," so the outpouring of the spirit is an outpouring of the spirit of Jesus. The prophetic spirit at work in Jesus is the same spirit at work in these apostles, so now, as we see, the apostles in the succeeding narrative, all of the protagonists in Acts—Peter, John, Stephen, Philip, Paul, all the people who fundamentally advanced the story—are portrayed by Luke in stereotypical fashion.

All of them are filled with the Holy Spirit, speak in the Holy Spirit; they proclaim boldly, they preach, they speak God's word, they do signs and wonders, and they create among the people either acceptance or rejection. The same characteristics that Luke ascribed to Jesus in the Gospel are here ascribed to his successors, the disciples. This is why Luke's portrayal of the disciples in his Gospel is not as negative as that in Mark, nor does he emphasize their intelligence as in Matthew. In Luke, the disciples are prophets in training, and when the Holy Spirit is poured out on them, then they continue to his message and his program, so that the first church in Jerusalem—we tend to call it the birth of the church at Pentecost, in Luke's terms—the birth of the church is the restoration of Israel for which Jesus worked.

Notice that at Pentecost you have Jews from all over the world who are in attendance because it is one of the great festivals of Judaism, and they're all there, so you have in effect Jews from the Diaspora, Jews from Jerusalem who are present, and the outpouring of the Holy Spirit on all flesh is interpreted at the sign of the resurrection and the exaltation of Jesus. And Peter's speech in Acts 2:1-37 concludes, notice, and I will read this: "Let the house of Israel therefore know assuredly that God has made him both Lord and Christ, this Jesus whom you crucified. Now when they heard this they were cut to the heart, and they said to Peter and the rest of the apostles, (the same thing that the people said to John the Baptist), 'Brethren, what should we do?'

"And Peter says, 'Repent, be baptized in the name of Jesus Christ for the forgiveness of your sins (notice, just as Jesus forgave sins, so they are to have their sins forgiven); and you shall receive the gift of the Holy Spirit.'" He concludes that exhortation by saying, "Save yourselves from this crooked generation." Peter said in the speech that they are to be saved, and what salvation means here is exactly what it meant in the Gospel, namely, to be part of this restored people. So the salvation then is not a matter of going to heaven; it's a matter of belonging to the restored Israel that Jesus had proclaimed, and now it is being realized.

What is the first thing that they do? Luke provides us our first summary of the life of this community in 2:41-47. I will read this:

"So those who received his word were baptized, and there were added that day about three thousand souls." Notice that what is happening here is that we have the formation of a community, so that's the saving. "And they devoted themselves to the apostles' teaching and fellowship, to the breaking of bread and the prayers." We recognize Lukan themes: teaching, fellowship, meals—breaking of bread and prayer. "And fear came upon every soul; and many wonders and signs were done through the apostles. And all who believed were together and had all things in common; they sold their possessions and goods and distributed them to all, as any had need. And day-by-day, attending the temple together and breaking bread in their homes, they partook of food with glad and generous hearts, praising God and having favor with all the people. And the Lord added to their number day by day those who were being saved."

There is no salvation outside the church, in other words, because the church is a definition of social reality. Salvation is to belong to that remnant people within Israel. It is striking, is it not? that the way they respond in repentance is exactly what John said they should do, share their possessions. It's exactly what Jesus said was the demand of discipleship, so they share all their possessions in common and give to everybody who has need. They thereby combine in interesting fashion both the giving up of their possessions and the giving of alms, so the community of possessions in some sense is the perfect realization of the prophets' program with respect to the use of possessions.

Notice the story that follows is the story of the healing of the lame man in the temple. Once more, Luke is concerned to show us that this is a continuation of Jesus's program of calling the outcasts. The lame man sits at the gate of the temple, he is prevented from participating in the cultic life of the temple, and so he begs alms from them, and Peter says to him, "Gold and silver I do not have, but what I have I will give you in the name of Jesus Christ of Nazareth. Walk," and he took him by the right hand, imitating Jesus, raised him up, and immediately his feet and ankles were made strong, and he goes leaping through the precincts of the temple praising God, so, in other words, this man has been restored to the cultic life of Israel. The community is meeting and praying in the temple precincts, as Jesus had done.

This is not a new religion; it is the restored spirit-filled prophetic program of Israel. Notice when Peter preaches on this occasion, when the leaders of the synagogue don't like this, as they didn't in the case of Jesus, so they call Peter and John to account, and this is in Acts 4:8, "Peter, filled with the Holy Spirit (note), says to them, 'Rulers of the people and elders, if we are being examined today concerning a good deed done to a cripple, by what means this man has been healed, be it known to you all and to the people of Israel that by the name of Jesus Christ of Nazareth, whom you crucified, whom God raised from the dead, by him this man is standing before you well. This is the stone which was rejected by you builders, but which has become the head of the corner. And there is salvation in no one else, for there is no other name under heaven given among men by which we must be saved.'"

In other words, Jesus is the prophet around whom the people must gather, so Peter calls this a sign of healing, and the sign is that healing restores the people; as the man is healed, the people are saved. In this narrative in Jerusalem, thousands of Jews join the community, and so they enjoy favor with all the people. It is only the leaders who oppose them. The ordinary people think that they are great, so this success, this spirit-filled success in Jerusalem addresses two major Lukan concerns.

First is this, that even though God's people, or mainly their leaders rejected God's first visitation—Jesus was rejected as prophet and killed—God remained faithful and provided another chance of repentance through the preaching of the apostles. In other words, in Acts, Jesus is the prophet whom God raised up that Moses had predicted, not simply by election but by being raised up. And how is Jesus powerfully present in Acts? Through the apostles who have his spirit, who do his deeds and proclaim his message, and therefore Israel has a second chance. God has proved faithful; God has overcome human rejection and been faithful to his promises, so Luke is writing his narrative about the things that God brought to fulfillment among us.

He wrote it in sequence because they had to see that the rejection of Jesus was not the end point, that there was another step to follow, and this is the second concern. Even though they had rejected Jesus, many of the Jews accepted the prophet whom God raised up, with the result that these Jews in Jerusalem—and this is why Luke emphasizes the thousands; there's a community that is substantial within that population—they become the authentic remnant of Israel so that the leadership of the Twelve is leadership over Israel, and the leadership of the Sanhedrin, the chief priests and the elders who reject the prophet, Luke takes every pain to show is a disqualified leadership. They no longer command the people, so the second time that they arrest the apostles they have to do it in secret because of fear of the people who are thronging to visit.

What is the theological point that Luke is making then? The theological point is that the mission to the Gentiles, especially as this is carried on by Paul, is not a replacement of Israel. It is rather continuous with a believing Israel. When Paul says in Acts 26:6 that all he is doing is representing the hope of Israel, he is not being a hypocrite. He rather is saying that from beginning to end God's longing is for this people Israel. The difference is that Israel is now made up of the prophetic people within Judaism and the prophetic people within the Gentile world, so that this is now the new Israel, if you will, or the authentic Israel is a better expression of that.

We also see that the apostles are portrayed as prophets who continue Jesus's radical manner of life in new circumstances. They share their possessions and they manifest servant leadership by their waiting on tables. Notice in Chapter 4, Verses 32-37, another of Luke's summaries, "The company of those who believed were of one heart and soul, and no one said that any of the things which he possessed was his own, but they had everything in common, and they took what they had and sold their fields and brought their possessions and put them at the feet of the apostles, and the apostles shared them out among others." Just as at the feeding of the 5,000, Jesus had the apostles distribute, and just as at the Last Supper Jesus said, "Your leadership should be like a servant at table," so here the apostles were in the middle of the distribution of possessions. Look also at Chapter 6, Verses 1-7, where the apostles are actually waiting on tables of the widows until the number of widows become too many and they have to extend that leadership, servant leadership, to others.

Secondly, the apostles pray at every moment of crisis, just as Jesus had done, and are empowered by the Holy Spirit, just as he was. A remarkable passage, Chapter 4, Verse 23, following; the apostles are just released from prison and they come together with the other apostles, and they pray to God, quoting Psalm 2 as an interpretation of what has happened to Jesus, "for truly in this city there were gathered together against thy holy servant Jesus, whom thou didst anoint, both Herod and Pontius Pilate, with the Gentiles and the peoples of Israel, to do whatever thy hand and thy plan had predestined," but now they ask for power to speak the word boldly and do signs and wonders, "And when they had prayed, the place in which they were gathered together was shaken; and they were all filled with the Holy Spirit and spoke the word of God with boldness." They pray and are empowered by the Holy Spirit. They are prophets in the same way that Jesus was.

They heal the outcasts of the people, as Jesus did, breaking the boundaries of separation and stigma created by sickness. In fact, their healing power is even greater than Jesus'. Luke notes in 5:12,

"Now many signs and wonders were done among the people by the hands of the apostles. More than ever believers were added to the Lord, multitudes, both of men and women, so that they even carried out the sick onto the streets, and laid them on beds and pallets, that as Peter came by even his shadow might fall on some of them. The people also gathered from the towns around Jerusalem, bringing the sick and those afflicted with unclean spirits, and they were all healed." They are doing exactly what Jesus had appointed them to do, which was to heal the outcasts.

Finally they bear witness boldly. Jesus is a prophet because he spoke of the word of God boldly before opposition and testified up to the end. The apostles are witnesses and they continue to bear witness boldly, even in the face of trial, persecution, and death. This is the importance of Paul's defense speeches from his arrest in Jerusalem all the way through storm at sea and shipwreck, to finally being in a house imprisonment in Rome at the very end of Acts, where he continues to proclaim notice to his fellow Jews that Jesus is the Messiah and the one whom they should heed if they want to belong to the restored people.

The final point I want to make on Luke-Acts is the way in which the church continues Jesus's radical program of table fellowship for the outcast through the bold initiative of including Gentiles without requiring of them circumcision and the observance of Torah. From a distance of 2,000 years, since Christians today are almost entirely Gentile in their ethnic makeup, there is a tendency to miss the enormity and the radical character of this most decisive decision in early Christianity because of course we Gentiles say, "Naturally God wanted Gentiles to be part of the people, and naturally we don't have to observe Jewish regulations and so forth and so on," but it was not obvious. In fact, all of the precedents of scripture, everything in Torah was on the side of the conservative Christians who demanded that if we're going to include Gentiles, then they have to keep the law and they have to be circumcised.

Why? Because Torah, which had thought of the people of Israel as the light of revelation to the Gentiles, "Gentiles can join, we want them to join, but by being proselytes, by converting and by taking on the yoke of Torah and observing Torah." When, through God's initiative, first Peter and then Paul and then others begin to convert Gentiles so that there's this massive demographic influx of new people, the decision is not whether or not God likes Gentiles—that's obvious, God has brought them into the people—the issue is one of how do we manage this in terms of tradition and, above all, in terms of table fellowship. Remember, the whole notion of being Jewish was to be separate, was to be holy, and this was marked by the observance of law, so that Jews could only eat with fellow Jews precisely because their practices marked them off as devoted to the one God of Israel.

Gentiles, by definition, will eat with anybody; that's the way they are—they have no separateness—so the liberals within early Christianity who said "Let's just let the Gentiles come in with no obligations at all," were not recognizing how difficult it is to deal with body symbolism, because it was easy for Gentiles to have table fellowship with Jews but it was impossible for Jews to have table fellowship with Gentiles and still be Jews. They were asked to give up their entire heritage for this initiative, and so Luke shows us in five dramatic chapters, in Chapters 10-15, how slowly humans caught up with God's initiative, how God first worked outside the people and gave a vision to Cornelius, who was a Gentile, and then to Peter, and they got together and compared notes and began to see that God was calling them to some greater initiative. Then this was challenged, and then anonymous Christians went off and converted Gentiles, and then Paul and Barnabas converted Gentiles.

Finally, we have the great scene in Acts 15, where the church comes together in council and makes this radical decision to accept Gentiles without requiring circumcision or the observance of Torah, so they followed God's initiative rather than the precedence of Torah. It was very radical, and what people failed to realize is that it was in direct continuity with Jesus's program of table openness, of accepting sinners and tax collectors, except the church was far more radical than Jesus. Jesus could only envisage the sinners among Israel. For Jews, Gentiles, by definition, are impure, are sinners, so this is a very radical gesture, a very radical act in which the church was more prophetic even than Jesus.

They made that decision through much anguish, so it was very hard to see where God was going, and it required that they made compromises. They made a compromise that Gentiles had to observe certain basic things, not that they became Jews but so that Jews could eat them. These are the basic observances that would enable Jews to have table fellowship with Gentiles. It's much harder to be a prophetic church within institutions and many, many people over generations than it is to be a prophetic messiah. Jesus was a prophet with a gang of 12 in the summer of love; it's kind of easy to be egalitarian under those circumstances. But to actually put this into action with large populations and over generations is a remarkable testimony to the power of Luke's vision of what Jesus's prophetic mission is really about.

Lecture Twenty-One
Gospel of John—Context of Conflict

Scope:

The full force of the synoptic interdependence is first realized when we appreciate how very different the Fourth Gospel (John) is in its version of Jesus's ministry, his speech, his acts, even his passion, death, and resurrection. Asking about the relationship between the Synoptics and John leads to the consideration of John's style, structure, and symbolism. What appears to be a simple and straightforward account of an eyewitness turns out to be something more complex and more interesting.

Outline

I. Although it is also a narrative Gospel, John (also FG = Fourth Gospel) stands apart from the Synoptic Gospels as a distinctive witness and interpretation.

   A. The basic facts of Jesus's ministry are different.
      1. His ministry is three years rather than one year and is focused in Judaea rather than Galilee.
      2. The cleansing of the temple is in a different place in the narrative; the time of Jesus's death is different, as is the character of the resurrection accounts.

   B. In the Fourth Gospel, the nature of Jesus's deeds is distinctive.
      1. In Mark, exorcisms signal the arrival of God's rule; John has no exorcisms.
      2. John has Jesus work seven "signs" of a highly symbolic character.

   C. In John, Jesus speaks in a manner different than in Matthew, Luke, and Mark.
      1. Jesus does not issue crisp aphorisms, tell parables, or have controversies that are settled by an authoritative saying.

2. In John, Jesus has controversies involving his identity that go on for a long time (see chs. 5–10), and he speaks in long, self-revelatory monologues.

D. In John, there is a different sense of eschatology: In the Synoptics, God's judgment is future; in John, the emphasis is on the present judgment effected through Jesus.

II. The question of the relationship of John and the Synoptics is not easily resolved.

A. There is no sign of literary dependence on the Synoptics, but there is a sharing in the traditions also used by the Synoptics.
1. John and the Synoptics have recognizably the same passion narrative, and a number of stories (in a new form) are found in both John and the Synoptics (see especially the multiplication of the loaves; the cleansing of the temple).
2. John and the Synoptics share the same range of titles for Jesus: king, prophet, Messiah, Son of God, Son of Man.

B. The Fourth Gospel can be seen as *supplemental* to the Synoptic tradition.
1. The traditional understanding of this is material: John's three-year account provides information not in the Synoptics' one-year narrative.
2. The relationship is rather functional: John makes explicit what is implicit in the Synoptic tradition.

III. The circumstances of John's composition are obscure, but the text reveals signs of conflict and developed reflection.

A. Some of John's language reflects a situation not during Jesus's lifetime but in the experience of the community (see chs. 3, 9, and 16).

B. The Gospel is remarkably candid about the deeper insight and interpretation that came about as a result of the resurrection and the presence of the paraclete (16:12–14; see 2:21–22; 12:16; 20:9).

C. Although it has roots in eyewitness testimony (19:35), therefore, the Gospel as it stands is the result of sustained reflection on the past in light of continuing experiences in the community.

D. Those experiences account at least in part for the sharp dualism found in the Fourth Gospel (and other literature associated with John): light and darkness, flesh and spirit, truth and falsehood are symbols that stand for a theological opposition (God/world) and social conflict (insider/outsider).

IV. The Fourth Gospel is at once straightforward and subtle, profound and provocative.

A. It is stylistically simple and structurally straightforward.

1. The prologue (1:1–18) announces themes and sets the pattern.

2. The Book of Signs (1:19–12:50) contains the public ministry of Jesus.

3. The Book of Glory (13:1–20:31) has Jesus's teaching of his followers (13:1–17:26) and the exaltation of Jesus through death and resurrection (18:1–20:31).

4. The epilogue (21:1–25) contains a final appearance of Jesus.

B. Yet everything in John contains at least two levels of meaning.

1. John is fond of words bearing double meanings: see "lifted up" (3:14) and "glory."

2. John appropriates the symbolism of Jewish feasts to express the identity of Jesus: Passover (2:13; 6:4; 12:12), Booths (7:1–10), and Hanukkah (10:22).

3. Characters in the story have a representative function: Martha, Nicodemus, Jesus, the Jews.

Essential Reading:
The Gospel of John.

Supplementary Reading:
L. T. Johnson, *The Writings of the New Testament*, pp. 525–557.

J. L. Martyn, *History and Theology in the Fourth Gospel.* 3rd ed. (Louisville: Westminster John Knox, 2003).

G. O'Day, *Revelation in the Fourth Gospel: Narrative Mode and Theological Claim* (Philadelphia: Fortress Press, 1986).

Questions to Consider:

1. Consider this proposition: "The character of the Synoptic tradition becomes clear only when it is compared to the Gospel of John."

2. How does the setting of separation from Judaism help account for the sharp dualism of John's Gospel?

Lecture Twenty-One—Transcript
Gospel of John—Context of Conflict

Over the next four lectures, we consider the Canonical Gospel that for many Christians is the most important Gospel. They think of the Gospel of John, or as often the Fourth Gospel, as true in a way distinct from the Synoptics because, in their view, it reveals Jesus's true character as divine. Many Christians today indeed are solidly Johannine Christians in their understanding of Jesus and of themselves. The Gospel of John will require of us a special approach, not only because of its undoubted beauty and power but because that beauty and power also has some troubling dimensions.

No more than with the Synoptic Gospels can we be confident about the time and place of composition. Assigning John the date 90 is somewhat arbitrary. It could be decades earlier than that; it could be a few years later than that. What is clear is that John's Gospel is shaped by the experience of conflict. We can begin to approach this special Canonical Gospel by means of comparison and contrast with the Synoptic Gospels taken as a whole. Although it is also a narrative gospel, it speaks of Jesus in the form of a story, John stands apart from the Synoptic Gospels as a distinctive witness and interpretation.

Let's begin with the basic facts of the ministry, which are different in John than in the Synoptics. In the Synoptic Gospels, Jesus's ministry lasts one year. In John's Gospel, it seems to last at least two and a half to three years. John reports Jesus as having been present at the Passover feast in Chapter 2, again in Chapter 6, and then finally at the moment of his death in Chapter 19. In the Synoptic Gospels, we get the impression that Jesus's ministry is centered in Galilee in the north of Palestine, and Jesus makes a single journey to Jerusalem and his death. In John's Gospel, the clear impression is given that Jesus centers his ministry in Judea, in the southern part of Palestine around Jerusalem and only makes occasional forays to Galilee and back.

Incidents take place in different locations in his narrative. John has a cleansing of the temple, but it occurs at the very beginning of Jesus's ministry in Chapter 2, Verses 13-25. In the Synoptics, you will recall, it is Jesus's cleansing of the temple which is the prophetic gesture that leads to his death. John puts it at the very beginning of the narrative. Indeed, speaking of Jesus's death, the date of his death is different in John's Gospel than in the Synoptics. In John's Gospel, it takes place a day earlier. Jesus is killed, the evangelist notes, on the day of preparation for the Passover. According to the Synoptics a few hours later, Jesus would have been eating the Passover supper with his followers, so there's a different dating that's going on.

Even the resurrection accounts have a different character in John. There is an empty tomb story, but it doesn't involve a bunch of women who go to the tomb. It's Mary who goes to the tomb by herself, then calls Peter and John, who have a footrace to the tomb, and that's how that story is constructed. Then we have an appearance to the disciples, but it is quite different than the one reported by Luke, another appearance in which so-called doubting Thomas is involved, which is absent from the Synoptic Gospels, and a final appearance of Jesus in Galilee when the disciples have decided to go fishing again; so each of these resurrection accounts is the same in terms of the convictions that they express, but are fashioned in different ways. That's the first point, the facts.

Secondly, in the Fourth Gospel the deeds of Jesus are distinctive. You will remember that in Mark's Gospel, exorcisms, driving out unclean spirits, were a major theme, as they were also in Matthew and Luke, as a sign of the in-breaking of God's kingdom. How remarkable that in John's Gospel there's not a single exorcism; no demons are driven out. Rather, John has Jesus work seven symbolic signs, *seemia*. Three of them are what we would call nature miracles, the changing of water into wine at the wedding feast of Cana in Chapter 2, the multiplication of loaves in Chapter 6, the walking on the water in Chapter 6. Then we have two healings: the healing of the paralytic in Chapter 5; the healing of the man born blind in Chapter 9; and climactically and most impressively, the raising from the dead, the resuscitation of Lazarus in Chapter 11, so a different set of miracles than in the Synoptics.

Thirdly, Jesus talks differently in John than he does in the Synoptics. In Matthew, Luke, and Mark, Jesus characteristically speaks in the form of short aphorisms, as we have seen. "Don't put your light under a bushel; let your light shine upon a hill; don't throw your pearls before swine." John has no such aphorisms. Or in the Synoptics, Jesus speaks in the form of parables, these marvelous brief metaphoric stories. Jesus does not speak in parables in John's Gospel. He does deliver himself of a few *paroimiai*, comparisons, or figures—the shepherd, the door of the sheep folds, the vine and the branches—but these brief comparisons are nothing like the parables of the prodigal son or the parables of the rich man Dives.

Nor in John does Jesus engage in brief vivid controversies with the Pharisees, such as we find in Mark and Luke and Matthew when they challenge him on some point of law and he rebukes them and rebuts them with a single snappy one liner, "The Son of manl is Lord, even of the Sabbath." Rather in John, the opponents won't go away. John has these long controversies that extend themselves over a fairly long period of time. Look, for example, at Chapters 5-10, which is almost entirely one long controversy between Jesus and his opponents. These controversies tend to merge into long, self-revelatory discourses or monologues on the part of Jesus, so Jesus's way of speaking is different, just as his way of acting is different in John's Gospel.

Fourth, John has a different sense of eschatology, or when God's judgment is. In the Synoptics, as we saw, God's judgment is entirely future. The Son of man will come on the clouds of heaven and receive dominion. Matthew showed us in Matthew 25 that magnificent vision of the Son of man sitting upon a throne and judging all of the nations. It's future. In John, we have some little indications of future eschatology, for example, in Chapter 5, Verses 28-29, but for the most part John has what scholars call a realized eschatology. God's judgment is taking place not in the future but in the ministry of Jesus itself. He is the light that has come into the world, and that light reveals who is in the light and who is in the darkness so that his coming is already a *krisis*, a judgment, a crisis. So John has put God's judgment into the ministry of Jesus himself. How people respond to Jesus is how they will be responded to by God, is how John works at this.

We are posed with a question, therefore, of the relationship between John and the Synoptic Gospels. Is there any way of relating these two gospel traditions? It's not easily resolved. The first thing that we can say is that there is no trace of literary dependence of John on the Synoptic Gospels. The linguistic evidence that we saw with Matthew, Mark, and Luke, which suggested that one was the source for the others, is lacking in the case of John. Even where there are similar materials, the wording is different, as in the multiplication of the loaves or the walking on the water or the passion account. But there is a sharing in the Synoptic tradition, so there's no Synoptic dependence, but there is a dipping into some of the same traditions that were used also by the Synoptic Gospels.

Most obviously, John has a recognizably same passion account, with variations that I will note later, and John has a number of stories that appear also in the Synoptics that he presents often in an altered form. I've already mentioned the cleansing of the temple, which he puts at the beginning of his Gospel. We also have the entry into the city in Chapter 12, Verses 12-19. John has a healing of a paralytic. In Mark, it's a paralytic who has to be let down through the roof by his friends; in John, in Chapter 5, it's a paralytic who can't get to the healing waters of a pool. John has Jesus healing an official's son, which looks remarkably like the healing of the centurion's servant in the Gospel of Luke, Chapter 7. And John has Jesus healing a blind man, much like the healing of the blind man in Mark, Chapter 8, so there are these shared stories that we can recognize.

John is working with the same stuff that the Synoptic Gospels are working with, and we could extend this by saying that in John we find the same titles ascribed to Jesus that we find in the Synoptic Gospels. He is called king, prophet, messiah, savior, son of God, even, remarkably, Son of manl. One of the distinctive things about the title Son of manl is that it's not found in Paul's letters or other New Testament writings; it is found only in the Gospels, and it is found only in the mouth of Jesus, or as ascribed to speech of Jesus. John continues that pattern; Jesus uses Son of man self-referentially. It is a designation that he gives himself. It is true that all of these designations are given to Jesus in John's Gospel, but we must be cautious and not transfer the meaning of those designations from the

Synoptics to John, so when John calls Jesus prophet, he does not necessarily have the same thing in mind with that title that we saw the Gospel of Luke had in calling Jesus prophet.

The Fourth Gospel is often seen as having a supplemental relationship to the Synoptics tradition, and there are two ways of defining the supplemental relationship, one an ancient and traditional one, and another which is more recent and is my own. The older way of viewing the supplemental character of John's Gospel is in terms of material; that is, John has a larger envelope in which to put Jesus's traditions. John has a three-year ministry, as we saw, so ancient readers thought of John's Gospel as simply filling in stuff that Jesus was doing in Judea, for example, that Matthew, Mark, and Luke didn't report. He supplements the Synoptic tradition by adding new materials because he has a more extended version of the good news. It seems to me that this doesn't carry us very far.

It seems to me that the relationship is rather a formal or functional one, and I put it this way: John makes explicit what is implicit in the Synoptic tradition. John's overriding tendency as a Gospel writer is to make everything explicit. The claims of Jesus, the claims that Jesus makes about God, are all put out on the table. I use the phrase explicit and implicit because I think that they are there in the Synoptic tradition, but they are not unfolded. They are folded into the story, so when Jesus in the Synoptics says, "The time has come; believe in the good news; the kingdom of God is at hand," he's saying in effect, "I know the mind of God. I am the messenger from God. I represent God." It's implicit; he's not simply making a scholarly observation. There's a claim that's implicit there. Or in the Gospel of Luke, when Jesus says, "The one who receives you receives me, and the one who receives me receives the one who sent me," there is again an implicit equation between the one sent out and the one sending.

But in John, all of this is made explicit. When Jesus multiplies the loaves in John's Gospel, as he does in the Synoptic Gospels, feeding the 5,000, it's only John who then has Jesus go on to say, "I am the bread of life; this is the bread that has come down from heaven." He makes the implications of being able to multiply food explicit. Or in Mark, we saw that Jesus heals a blind man, but only in John does

Jesus go on to say, "I am the light of the world." It's quite clear in the Synoptics that the way people respond to Jesus is meant to imply the way they respond to God. In John, this is made utterly explicit, so what we find then is that John's Gospel is working with the Synoptic traditions but raises them to a level of explicitness. John truly is a theological narrative in that the work of God is made explicit in the stories about Jesus.

Let's turn to what we can learn about the circumstances of John's composition and what this might tell us about the shape of John's Gospel. Some of John's language reflects a situation not during Jesus lifetime but in the experience of John's community. John is quite candid about this. At some level, just as John is explicit about the claims of Jesus, so it's remarkably candid and transparent about the process of gospel formation. Let's start with Jesus in his farewell discourse to his followers at the Last Supper, in Chapter 16, Verses 1-4. "I have said all this to you to keep you from falling away. They will put you out of the synagogues; indeed, the hour is coming when whoever kills you will think he is offering service to God. And they will do this because they have not known the Father, nor me. But I have said these things to you, that when their hour comes you may remember that I told you of them." So John has the warning of Jesus to what is going to happen later on to them.

But notice here in Chapter 9, long before Chapter 16, we have Jesus has healed the man born blind. The leaders confront his parents. They say, "Don't ask us. Ask the man (we'll return to this story later on; he's old enough to talk). His parents said this (I'm in 9:22) because they feared the Jews, for the Jews had already agreed that if any one should confess him to be Christ, he was to be put out of the synagogue." Therefore, his parents said he is of age; ask him. We have the situation in which what's supposed to be happening in the future is retrojected back into the time of Jesus himself.

Notice also the statement of Jesus then in Chapter 14, "These things I have spoken to you while I am still with you, but the counselor, the Holy Spirit whom the father will send in my name, he will teach you all things and bring to your remembrance all that I have said to you." Again, the spirit is going to come after Jesus's departure and lead to deeper insight into what has happened in the ministry of Jesus. Again, in Chapter 16:12-14, "I have yet many things to say to you, but you cannot bear them now. When the spirit of truth comes, he will guide you into all truth." They will have deeper insight later than they had while Jesus was still with them. We find a sense of this bifocal character of John's narrative. It's the story of Jesus, but it's also the story of what they are experiencing in Jesus's conversation with Nicodemus in Chapter 3.

This is a story about Jesus and a man who came to see him at night. They are talking to each other. The pronouns are singular, you and I, and all of a sudden, when Jesus says, "Are you a teacher of Israel, and yet you do not understand this?" (you singular), in 3:11, all of a sudden the language says, "Truly, truly, I say to you all (you plural), we speak of what we know and bear witness to what we have seen, but you all don't receive our testimony," and then the next verse, back to the singular. This is like a little window into the world of the Johannine community. It is not simply Jesus and a Jew, Nicodemus, of the past who don't understand each other. It's also the Johannine community speaking to the fellow Jews who have kicked them out of the synagogue who don't grasp what they're talking about, so John has this sort of layered character.

The Gospel is remarkably candid about the deeper insights and interpretations that come about as a result of the resurrection and the presence of the Paraclete. Look for example at Chapter 2, Verses 21-22. This is the story of the cleansing of the temple, which takes place, as I said, at the beginning of Jesus's ministry. Obviously, it creates a commotion. He's challenged by the Jews, and Jesus answers them, "Destroy this temple and in three days I will raise it up." The Jews then said, "It's taken 46 years to build this temple, and will you raise it up in three days?"

Here is the narrator giving us an authorial commentary in a way different than Matthew did. "But he spoke," John now addresses the reader, "But he spoke of the temple of his body. When therefore he was raised from the dead, his disciples remembered that he had said this, and they believed the scripture and the word that Jesus had spoken." This is a wonderful summary of the process of gospel formation. Something happened in the past, but after the resurrection the disciples see what had happened in light of the resurrection, in light of the interpretation of scripture, in light of the words and deeds that Jesus had spoken.

This is not the only example of this kind of reflection. We find as well when Jesus enters into the city on a donkey. This is in Chapter 12, Verse 12, following: "The next day a great crowd who had come to the feast heard that Jesus was coming to Jerusalem. So they took branches of palm trees and went out to meet him, crying, 'Hosanna! Blessed is he who comes in the name of the Lord, even the King of Israel!' And Jesus found a young ass and sat upon it; as it is written." Notice, this is the same text as used by Matthew, "Fear not, daughter of Zion; behold, your king is coming, sitting on an ass's colt!" But notice John's authorial commentary. His disciples did not understand this at first, but when Jesus was glorified, that is, after his death, then they remembered that this had been written of him and had been done to him, so there is a deeper memory when Jesus is raised.

Finally, at the empty tomb account, Simon Peter and John run to the tomb, they see that it's empty, but there are cloths left behind. Peter went in, he saw and believed, for as yet they did not know the scripture that he must rise from the dead. This understanding from scripture comes only after the resurrection. Although this Gospel may have roots in an eyewitness testimony—indeed, Chapter 19, Verse 35, at the moment of Jesus's death, there is a claim to eyewitness testimony on the part of a beloved disciple—the Gospel as it stands is a result of sustained reflection on the past in light of continuing experiences within the community.

We see this again quite explicitly in what is probably the first ending of John's Gospel in Chapter 20, Verses 30-31. "Jesus did many other signs in the presence of the disciples, which are not written in this book. But these are written that you may believe that Jesus is the Christ, the son of God, and, that believing, you may have life in his name." Two things about this first conclusion to the Gospel that I want to point out. The first is its candor that these things were selected and shaped in order to accomplish a certain end. The second is that the best Greek manuscripts have the present tense of believing, that you may go on believing. Like other gospels, John has not written for purposes of evangelization, to make people Christians; it is written for purposes of reinforcement for those who already have belief.

These experiences of conflict and these experiences of being kicked out of the synagogue account at least in part for the sharp dualism found in the Fourth Gospel and other literature associated with John, the Book of Revelation and the three letters of John. We have lined up in sharp polarity light and darkness, flesh and spirit, truth and falsehood. These literary symbols stand for a theological opposition, God-world, which also have a social referent, namely, us and them. So we can line them up in columns. On one side is light and truth and spirit and God and us, and on the other side you have darkness, flesh, falsehood, the devil, and outsiders.

The Fourth Gospel, in conclusion, is at once straightforward and subtle, profound and provocative. Stylistically, it is utterly simple. John has the simplest Greek in the New Testament. It's what I assign to first-year Greek students to read. It is schoolboy Greek; it's very simple and straightforward, relatively correct, and structurally it's straightforward. Look how it unfolds; you have a prologue in Chapter 1, Verses 1-18, that announces themes and sets a basic pattern for the Gospel, then what scholars call the Book of Signs from 1:19 to 12:50, which contains all of the public ministry of Jesus. It's called the Book of Signs because here's where Jesus does the seven wonders, and the controversies that they engender. We will look at that more closely next lecture.

Thirdly, the Book of Glory, Chapter 13:1 to 20:31, which falls into two parts. First, the teaching of Jesus to his disciples in Chapters 13-17; all of Jesus's teaching to his followers is found in those chapters, none of it in the earlier chapters—John has a very different system of organization—and then what John calls the exaltation or glorification of Jesus through his death and resurrection, Chapters 18:1 to 20:31. Then we have the strange second ending of John's Gospel. I already read you the first ending, but we have the epilogue in Chapter 21:1-25, which contains a final appearance of Jesus to his disciples and takes care of the question of what happened to Peter and John. That concludes finally with this second ending. "There are also many other things which Jesus did; were every one of them to be written, I suppose that the world itself could not contain the books that would be written," and of course this course is all about all the books that could be written about Jesus.

John's Gospel is at one level stylistically simple and structurally very straightforward, public, private exaltation. Yet, everything in John contains at least two levels of meaning. John's Gospel continues to intrigue simple and sophisticated readers alike because it is at one level utterly transparent—it says everything up front—and yet it keeps on revealing layers of itself. John, for example, is very fond of double meanings of words, words like lifted up, "the Son of man will be lifted up," which means (a) he will be executed, he will be lifted up on the cross, but (b), it means also he will be exalted. Likewise, John loves to play on words like glory, *doxa*, so that at one level the word doxa, which in ordinary Greek means opinion or reputation, it has that meaning. However, the word doxa can also be used for God's presence among humans. For example, the end of Chapter 12, people prefer one kind of doxa to the other kind of doxa, and that's their problem. He uses these double levels.

He appropriates the symbolism of Jewish feasts to express the identity of Jesus—Passover, the feast of booths, the feast of Hanukkah—so that at one level Jesus seems to be saying very straightforward things; at another level he's appropriating to himself the symbols associated with those Jewish feasts. We'll examine that in some detail in a later lecture. And finally, characters in John's story also have a polyvalent function; they represent themselves and something else. When Martha says to Jesus, "I believe that you are the Messiah, the son of God," she represents the ideal believer. Nicodemus represents the befuddled Jew who is sincere but can't quite get it. Pilate represents malevolent political authority. Jesus represents God. The bad news is that the Jews have to play the role of the disbelieving world and therefore of the enemies of God. We'll talk about those difficulties in a later presentation.

Lecture Twenty-Two
Gospel of John—Jesus as the Man From Heaven

Scope:

John's prologue (1:1–18) establishes the basic dramatic scenario of this most dramatic Gospel: Jesus is not simply a Jewish teacher but the word of God who has entered fully into human flesh. His wonders are "signs" of God's presence. He is the light that enters a world of darkness and, by revealing light, also brings judgment on those who prefer darkness to light. This presentation considers John's powerful portrait of Jesus, which combines a constant insistence on his full humanity, while also portraying him as the revelation of God.

Outline

I. In place of a genealogy or birth account, John's prologue (1:1–18) serves to identify Jesus as the one who has come from God to dwell with humans and to establish basic themes of the Gospel.

   A. Jesus is the word who exists from the beginning with God (1:1–2) and who "became flesh" (1:14) in order to reveal God's glory (= presence) in humanity.

   B. The prologue contrasts light and darkness, God and world, those who accept and those who reject, law and grace/truth; it also provides the Gospel's pattern of descent and ascent (see 1:18).

   C. The prologue contains two interruptions about John the Baptist, who is identified as a witness to the light.

   D. The Gospel of John names Jesus as God.

II. The narrative sequence following the prologue shows the subtlety of John's literary art.

   A. In content, 1:19–51 serves as the equivalent of the Synoptics' "Calling of the Disciples." But in John, the process is one of mutual naming, in which Jesus's identity is unfolded for the reader.

B. The story of the Wedding at Cana is dramatic in its own right, but when read within the sequence of "days" noted in 1:1, 29, 35, 43, and 2:1, the reader understands that "the first of Jesus' signs" (2:11) also reveals the first seven days of the new creation.

III. The Book of Signs (1:19–12:50) is dominated by the public wonders worked by Jesus and the controversies with his opponents that they generate.

A. John has Jesus work seven "signs": changing water into wine (2:1–11), healing an official's son (4:36–53), healing a paralytic (5:2–9), feeding the multitude (6:1–13), walking on water (6:16–21), healing a man born blind (9:1–12), and raising Lazarus from the dead (11:17–44).

B. Throughout his public ministry, Jesus is identified by outsiders and believers with a variety of titles.

   1. His enemies claim he has a demon and is a Samaritan (7:20; 8:48).

   2. The crowd names Jesus as "Messiah" and "Prophet" and "King"; in John, each of these designations has some level of truth, and each reveals something of contemporary messianic expectations.

   3. Believers call Jesus Messiah and Son of God, Savior of the world, Holy One of God, and even "God."

C. Distinctive to John is the consistent way in which Jesus also names himself.

   1. As in the Synoptics, Jesus uses the title "Son of Man" of himself but in a distinctive manner.

   2. In the Synoptics, this title is connected with Jesus's future glory and present suffering.

   3. In John, this title is connected with the notion of Jesus as "the man from heaven."

   4. Jesus also designates himself by a series of "I am" statements connected to metaphors (corresponding to his signs): bread of life (6:35), light of the world (8:12), door of the sheep (10:7), good shepherd (10:11), true vine

(15:1), resurrection and life (11:25), the way and the truth and the life (14:6).

5. Most dramatic are the absolute "I am" statements that echo the self-identification of God in Torah (8:58; 18:6; see Exod. 3:14; Isa. 41:4).

IV. The Book of Signs concludes with a dramatic recap of Jesus's ministry in which the crisis is posed in terms of a choice (and a judgment) between light and darkness, between the approval of humans and the presence of God (12:27–50).

Essential Reading:

The Gospel of John, 1–6.

Supplementary Reading:

W. A. Meeks, "The Man from Heaven in Johannine Sectarianism," *Journal of Biblical Literature* 91 (1972): 44–72.

D. M. Ball, *"I Am" in John's Gospel: Literary Function, Background, and Theological Implications* (JSNTSsup 124; Sheffield: Sheffield Academic Press, 1996).

Questions to Consider:

1. How does John reinforce the "insider" character of his narrative by the way in which characters "name" Jesus?

2. How does John communicate that God's judgment is present in the ministry of Jesus?

Lecture Twenty-Two—Transcript
Gospel of John—Jesus as the Man From Heaven

In the previous lecture, I showed some of the ways in which the Fourth Gospel is distinctive in its depiction of Jesus's ministry and in its literary configuration. We saw that it is a layered composition that is even more explicit about its reflectiveness than the Synoptic Gospels are. In John, the resurrection perspective that is implicit in all the Gospels is more pervasively and explicitly present. The evangelist is quite candid about the fact that the resurrection of Jesus and the gift of the Holy Spirit, which John calls the *paraclete*, has shaped the telling of the story and that the story therefore really is a theological narrative that makes explicit the Christian convictions about who Jesus was. In this presentation, I want to look more closely at the Jesus as the man from heaven in John's Gospel.

We begin at the beginning. We've paid a particular attention in each of the Gospels to the way in which it begins, as giving us clues as to the character of the Gospel. We saw Mark's abrupt and highly mysterious beginning perfectly fit his presentation of Jesus as the mystery of the kingdom of God whom nobody can fully grasp. In Matthew, we saw the genealogy, which conveyed Matthew's concern to connect Jesus to the heritage of Abraham and of Israel. And in Luke we saw the use of the prologue, which gave us clues as to the problem of theodicy that Luke's composition was trying to address; namely, is God faithful to God's promises? John gives us in place of a genealogy or a birth account another kind of prologue.

It's not a prologue, like Luke's, that tells the reader what kind of work this is going to be. Rather, it begins with poetry, and it begins with an allusion to the absolute beginning of all things, the first words of the Bible, "In the beginning." The prologue serves to identify Jesus as the one who has come from God to dwell among humans, and the prologue serves to establish certain basic themes of the Gospel. Everybody wants to hear about the prologue, and I'm no exception. This is one of the most beautiful passages in John's Gospel. It has provoked perhaps the most theological speculation in the history of

Christianity and we deserve to have it read out loud and to look at some of its dimensions.

"In the beginning was the Word, and the Word was with God, and the Word was God." It's quite clear that John deliberately begins with the phrase *"en arche"* with a cross- reference to the Book of Genesis so that what he's saying about the word, who is to be identified with Jesus, is to put him in the beginning with God, much as Jewish speculation about wisdom that we talked about in earlier lectures put Torah, or wisdom, at the beginning before creation in God's mind; likewise, John makes the statement about Jesus, "In the beginning was the Word, and the Word was with God, and the Word was God."

"He was in the beginning with God; all things were made through him, and without him was not anything made that was made." Once more, as with Jewish speculation about wisdom and Torah, namely, that wisdom was God's partner in creation, so John ascribes that elevated role to Jesus. So from the beginning Jesus is not simply a man from Nazareth; he is this word that has entered into humanity. "In him was life, and the life was the light of humans. The light shines in the darkness, and the darkness has not overcome it." The themes of life and light which are going to run through John's Gospel are here connected from the beginning with this word of God which was at work in creation itself.

In Verse 6 of the prologue, we find the first of two interruptions, if you will. Indeed, many scholars think that these perhaps were added by the evangelist to an earlier poem that did not have them. They are interjections dealing with John the Baptist. "There was a man sent from God, whose name was John. He came for testimony, to bear witness to the light, that all might believe through him. He was not the light, but came to bear witness to the light." We have seen that one of the things that all the Gospel writers struggle with is how to connect John to Jesus without overwhelming Jesus or diminishing John. In this case, the writer of John's Gospel has put John into the closest possible connection with Jesus, indeed, the divine word, but has identified him not as the light but as a witness to the light, so he has effectively relativized John's status even as he elevates John's status.

Verse 9 returns to that light. "The true light that enlightens every man was coming into the world. He was in the world, and the world was made through him, yet the world knew him not," so here we have the drama of acceptance and rejection. The very word through which God has created the world is not recognized by the world, so we have this theme of light and darkness, which becomes in John this theme of deliberate darkening or *scotosis*, the choice not to see, which is something quite else than being blind. Verse 11, "He came to his own," this translation has "home," but in Greek it's simply, "He came to his own," and it means his own people, "and his own people received him not." Jesus is going to be rejected by the very people among whom God's Torah and wisdom had been revealed in the Old Testament.

In contrast to those who did not receive the light, "to all who received him (Verse 12), who believed in his name, he gave power to become children of God; who were born (these people), not of blood nor of the will of the flesh nor of the will of man, but of God," so as he is from God, so those who believe in him are also born of God. It's a high claim. Verse 14 is justifiably recognized as the climax of the prologue, and it brings us down from the heights of the word's existence with God into humanity. It is a mythic descent. "And the Word became flesh and dwelt among us, full of grace and truth; we have beheld his glory, glory as of the only Son from the Father." It's an astonishingly rich statement.

First of all, notice that in Judaism, wisdom or Torah came to dwell among humans. Remember we made the connection between Torah and the Shekinah, the divine presence. John's language here about tempting or dwelling among us alludes to the divine presence in the Shekinah, so just as the Torah made the divine presence available to humans, in an even more dramatic fashion this word became actual flesh, became human, and tempted among us, so Jesus is the new place of God's presence among humans.

Therefore, we have two things which reflect this. First, he is full of grace and truth. Although these words are in Greek, they clearly allude to the two characteristics of Yahweh, the Lord in the Old Testament, *emeth va chesed*, which can be translated as "truth and grace," so this word become flesh is full of grace and truth. It is really the divine presence, and in case we miss that, "and we have beheld his glory, doxa," so the word *doxa* in the Septuagint, the Greek translation of the Old Testament, consistently translates *kabod*, or the divine presence, so what have we seen? Not simply reputation doxa, or opinion doxa, but the divine luminous presence among us, doxa. Jesus is said to be here the very embodied presence of God. It's no wonder that Christian theologians have turned to this passage when arguing about the divinity of Christ.

Once more, in Verse 15 then, after that high point, the author alludes to John. "John bore witness to him, and cried, 'This is the one of whom I said, `He who comes after me ranks before me, for he was before me.'" Again, John's status over against Jesus is nicely stated. Then in Verse 16, we return to the Word, "and from his fullness we have all received." I make mention of the word fullness because it is the Greek word *pleroma*; this word will be extensively employed by Gnostic Gospels in their speculations about what is this pleroma, what is this fullness, but that's in a later presentation. We have received from his fullness grace upon grace, "For the law was given through Moses; grace and truth came through Jesus Christ." Notice again grace and truth, the words for the very identity of God.

Then the prologue concludes with this remarkable statement, first, of the infinite qualitative distance between God and humans. No one has ever seen God, so humans don't see God. In effect, not even Moses saw God, so in order for humans to come into contact with God, God has to make the movement. He says, "The only son who is in the bosom of the father, he has made him known." The Greek text *exegesato*, has the sense of he has interpreted or made known God to humans. The reading, the only son, is found in many manuscripts; perhaps the harder reading in some Greek manuscripts, and maybe therefore the better reading, is that John has created a powerful oxymoron here by actually saying the only God who is in the bosom of the father has made God known and has named Jesus even as theos, or God, already in this prologue.

The prologue then of John's Gospel is poetry—we can arrange it in chiastic strokes—which has prose interjections concerning John the Baptist, but no reader of John's Gospel from the beginning can have any doubt as to the exalted status of Jesus as having come from God—he is the man from heaven par excellence—or about the exalted status of those who have received the light, who have chosen not to live in darkness and who accept the grace and truth that have come from him. Notice that the prologue establishes this basic pattern of descent from God to earth and ascent back. He is the one who is going to return to the father, so the prologue sets a quite remarkable stage for John's narrative, quite unlike any of the other Gospels.

If we look at the narrative sequence following the prologue, we catch a glimpse of the subtlety of John's literary arts. Let's look first at John 1:19-51. This is a sequence which is roughly equivalent to the Synoptic Gospels' calling of the disciples. You will remember in Mark and in Matthew and Luke, Jesus goes by the seaside and calls the fishermen, he goes by the tax collector's booth, and calls his disciples in that fashion. This is the rough equivalence here, but what happens in John is that as people become Jesus's disciples, they identify Jesus and Jesus identifies them. There is a kind of a mutual naming that goes on between Jesus and those whom he calls. It begins with John the Baptist. John says, "I am the voice of one crying in the wilderness. Make straight the way of the Lord, as the prophet Isaiah said." Notice that in the Synoptic Gospels they quoted Isaiah; here it's John himself who says, "I'm the guy, I am the voice of the one crying in the wilderness."

But as he's standing there with his disciples, and John is quite explicit about John having disciples of his own, he sees Jesus coming toward him—this is in 1:29—and says, "Behold the Lamb of God, who takes away the sin of the world." We have here the first allusion to the Passover, to the Lamb of God who bears the sin of the world. John says, "This is the one who baptizes with the Holy Spirit, and I have seen and I have born witness this is the son of God." John does not leave us in mystery or confusion about who Jesus is. It's all out there from the beginning. John says, "This is the son of God."

Then as he's standing with two of his disciples, again he identifies Jesus as the Lamb of God, and as a result he loses disciples. His disciples go off and follow Jesus, and Jesus sees them and he says, "What do you seek?" and they say "Rabbi (which means teacher), where are you staying?" and he says, "Come and see." This is marvelous; Jesus is the light coming into the world. "Where are you staying? Where are you?" "Come and remain with me." Later in John's farewell discourse, we will see the language about where are you going, where are you really, and what does it mean to remain in Jesus, but all of that double meaning is embedded already early on in his narrative.

They go on further and they say, "We have found the Messiah," which means Christ, another title of Jesus, and then Philip finds Nathaniel, and this is in Verse 45, "We have found him of whom Moses and the law and also the prophets wrote, Jesus of Nazareth, the son of Joseph," another designation. Nathaniel identifies him in Verse 49, "Rabbi, you are the son of God; you are the King of Israel." Even as Jesus is gathering these disciples, the reader is being introduced to the entire range of designations available for a messiah—rabbi, teacher, son of God, messiah, the son of Joseph, king of Israel. Everything's out in the open from the very beginning in John's narrative.

This passage concludes with Jesus giving his own self-identification. Jesus says "Because I said that I saw you under the fig tree (this is Nathaniel under the fig tree), do you believe? You shall see greater things than these," and he said to him, "Truly, truly, I say to you, you will see heaven opened, and the angels of God ascending and descending upon the Son of man." This is an allusion to the story in Genesis about Jacob and the house of God, where he sees the angels ascending and descending on the ladder, and he says, "This truly is the house of God." Here we have Jesus is the Son of man on whom angels descend and ascend, once more the pattern of coming down and going back, which is central to the movement of the myth in John's Gospel.

So we have here this opening section which appears to be straightforward but actually is a quite complex set of namings. It reaches a conclusion with the first of Jesus's signs. It is an odd story; it's the wedding feast at Cana. Once more, it appears to be somewhat arbitrary. Jesus and the disciples and his mother are invited to a wedding feast in Cana. While he's there, they run out of wine. His mother says, "They've run out of wine." He says, "Why are you bothering me?" His mother says, "Go do whatever he says," and Jesus says, "Fill these pitchers, these jugs, these jars full of water," huge jars, and they do, and he says, "Go draw from them," and they draw, and it turns out to be terrific wine, and the wine steward says, "This is amazing, because most of the time people serve the good wine first and then when people are drunk they serve the bad wine." He said, "You saved the good wine for last."

What's this about, changing water into wine, and why? And then John ends the story with quite a remarkable statement. He said "This was the first of the signs." Remember, we said that John uses the word *seemion*, sign, for the deeds that Jesus does. This is the first of his signs Jesus did at Cana in Galilee, and his disciples believed in him, so we have here a connection clearly to those who believed in him in the prologue, so this is what's going on here, and Jesus manifested his glory, so the word became flesh, and we saw his glory in the prologue, and here he does this sign, and they see his glory and believe in him. And then he went down to Capernaum with his mother and his brothers and disciples and they stay there for a few days.

What's going on here is fascinating. This wedding feast is dramatic in its own right, but why not read this in the sequence of John's narrative as he has invited us to read? Please notice the otherwise inexplicable note of days in 1:29, "The next day he saw Jesus coming toward him." In 1:35, the next day again, John was standing with two of his disciples. In 1:43, the next day, Jesus decided to go to Galilee, and then in 2:1, on the third day, there was a wedding feast at Cana. In the Christian lexicon, the third day refers to the resurrection, so Jesus's new life from old life, not Jesus's natural life but Jesus's resurrected life, the third day, so the wedding feast of Cana has something to do with new possibilities of life, not water but wine, and there's going to be clear Eucharistic symbolism for John's readers in this who are familiar with associating wine with the death and resurrection of Jesus as they celebrate the Lord's Supper, but there's more.

John begins in the beginning, day one, the next day, the next day, the next day, and after three days we have seven days, which correspond to the seven days of creation, but now it is the seven days of the new creation and in this subtle fashion, because there's no other reason for John to note the next day, the next day, the next day after the third day. This is a totally literary construction, which concludes with "they saw his glory," so we are clearly intended to understand that the word through whom God made all things has become flesh and that the deeds of Jesus are therefore the revelation of the new creation that is happening, the transformation of human existence through this person Jesus, who is God's word, so this is an example of how subtly John uses symbolism which could pass us by completely as we're reading because it does seem so very straightforward and pedestrian. Something quite else is going on here.

If we move from this opening to the rest of the Book of Signs, which extends from Chapter 1:19 to 12:50, we see that this first part of John's Gospel is dominated by the public wonders worked by Jesus and the controversies with his opponents that they generated. John in this section works seven signs: changing the water into wine, as we have seen; healing an official's son; healing a paralytic; feeding the multitude; walking on water; healing a man born blind; and then raising Lazarus from the dead, an incident which brings him great notoriety and leads eventually then to his rejection and death. But as he does these signs, Jesus is also being identified by various people, just as we saw in that opening sequence. John has everybody naming Jesus all the time, so both outsiders and believers with a variety of titles.

It's sort of like we see what's happening, but what went on? Who is this that's doing this? And so we have this process of trying to name what can't be named. So his enemies, not surprisingly, who are constantly engaging him in controversy after each one of these signs, claim that he's a demon or, worse, he's a Samaritan, so he's something alien; he's not one of us. The crowd names Jesus; they name him as messiah, prophet, king, and in John each of these designations has some level of truth and reveals something about contemporary messianic expectations, and I'll return to that in a later lecture. People who come to belief in John's Gospel get closer to the reality. They call him Lord, Messiah, son of God, savior of the world, holy one of God, and even remarkably, at the end, doubting Thomas calls Jesus "My Lord and my God," so that one can scarcely get a more exalted set of identifiers for Jesus.

But what is distinctive to John's Gospel is the way in which Jesus names himself, because in John's Gospel we always have these layers; it's like an onionskin. You've got the opponents, you've got the bystanders, you've got the believers, but at the heart of everything is what Jesus does and what Jesus says about himself, which is the deepest level of truth. Every level has some element of truth, but what Jesus says about himself is most true, three kinds of self-designations that I want to touch on. As in the Synoptics, Jesus refers to himself as the Son of man. In the Synoptics, we saw that the title Son of man was largely connected to Jesus's future glory and present suffering.

In John, the title Son of man is very much connected to this notion of Jesus as the man from heaven. You will see the angels ascending and descending on the Son of man or, in John, Chapter 6, Verse 62, after he multiplies the loaves and his opponents murmur because he has multiplied the loaves and said that he is the bread of life, Jesus, knowing in himself that his disciples murmured at it, said to them, "Do you take offense at this? Then what if you were to see the Son of man ascending where he was before?" The Son of man language in John is one in which the one who is going to come has already come. In the Synoptics, the Son of man is coming down; in John he's come down and is going back.

Jesus also designates himself by a variety of "I am" statements, which are metaphorical in character and are connected to the signs that he has done. He multiplies the loaves and then in 6:35 says, "I am the bread of life." He heals a blind man and in 8:12 he says, "I am the light of the world." He says, "I am the door of the sheep… I am the good shepherd… I am the true vine… I am the resurrection and the life," and then climactically, "I am the way and the truth and the life" in Chapter 14:6. All of these "I am's," seven in number, correspond to the seven signs that reveal Jesus's glory.

The most dramatic self-designations of Jesus are those where he doesn't attach "I am" to a metaphor but simply says, "I am" absolutely. All scholars here see an allusion to Exodus, Chapter 3:14, the burning bush, "Who are you, Lord?" which is translated in the Septuagint, "I am who am," or the Book of Isaiah, Chapter 41, Verse 4, in which Yahweh identifies himself as the great I am, so we have Jesus when he walks on the water and his disciples are frightened and he cries out to them, "I am. Don't be afraid," and in controversy with his opponents, particularly in Chapter 8, Verse 58—he's been in controversy with them for a considerable period of time—and he says—he's making claims about his father glorifying him—and he says that Abraham "rejoiced to see my day, and he saw it and was glad," which is kind of a remarkable statement.

Abraham, living a millennium ago, saw Jesus's day and saw it and was glad, and the Jews said to him, "You are not yet 50 years old, and you have seen Abraham?" and Jesus said to them, "Truly, truly, I say to you, before Abraham was, I am," and quite clearly there Jesus is making a statement of identity with God, and we find the climactic example of this in Chapter 18:6, when Jesus is in the garden and they are arresting him and he says, "Whom do you seek?" and they say, "Jesus of Nazareth," and Jesus said to them, "I am," and they fall back in fear, so clearly this "I am" language is meant to be theophoric, meant to reveal Jesus as God.

The Book of Signs concludes with a dramatic recap of Jesus's ministry in which the crisis is posed in terms of a choice and a judgment between light and darkness, between the approval of humans and the presence of God. This passage deserves quoting in extenso, but let me just pick up the final statement concerning Jesus's work among his fellow Jews. "Nevertheless, even many of the authorities believed in him, but for fear of the Pharisees they did not confess it, lest they should be put out of the synagogue (that theme again): for they loved the praise of men more than the praise of

God." Here John uses the word *doxa* in that double meaning that I have suggested. They loved human opinion more than they loved good opinion from God or, more decisively, they preferred good opinion from humans to the very presence and power of God, God's doxa that has been revealed through the humanity of Jesus.

Lecture Twenty-Three
Gospel of John—Jesus as Obedient Son

Scope:

If in John's drama Jesus represents God, then Jesus's opponents (whom John tends to call simply the Jews) represent enemies of God. Consequently, John's Gospel has sometimes been considered the most anti-Semitic New Testament composition. The complex ways in which this Gospel engages the world of Judaism are considered in this presentation. How should we evaluate the way in which, even as this Gospel asserts that "salvation comes from the Jews," it portrays actual Jews as blind to the light and resistant to God's claims?

Outline

I.   The powerful poetry of the Fourth Gospel has had a powerful effect, both positive and negative, on readers.

    A. For Christian theologians, John is the great source of doctrine concerning Jesus, precisely because of the explicitness of its propositions: "God so loved the world as to send his only son" (3:16).

    B. For mystics and ordinary believers alike, John's Jesus is the deep heart of the Christian reality: They think of the Gospel as having a Synoptic plot but a Johannine character.

    C. The negative effect is more subtle, and that is the tendency, when John's Gospel is made the center of Christian consciousness, to cultivate a sectarian attitude hostile to outsiders.

    D. Above all, John's Gospel is one of the main sources for the strain of anti-Semitism running through Christian theology.

II. The other side of the coin is that John's Jesus is, in many respects, the most intensely human in all the Gospels.

    A. It is a natural tendency to focus only on the "divine" dimensions of Jesus in the Fourth Gospel. Because Jesus "represents" God in the drama, his actions and speech seem to hover over the surface.

B. In the Fourth Gospel, Jesus's humanity is displayed in two significant ways:

    1. Jesus experiences fatigue (4:6) and anguish (12:27; 13:21); he weeps at the death of a friend (11:33–35); changes his mind (7:1–10); converses with real people in real places—they answer back!—(see 4:7–26); shows suspicion (2:24–25) and irritation (2:4; 6:26); and has real friends (11:1–12:9).

    2. Jesus is also, as human obedient to God, doing and saying what he is commanded by the Father: "I do not seek my own will, but the will of the one who sent me" (5:19–30).

III. John's relationship with Judaism, similarly, is extraordinarily complex, having positive and negative features.

A. John's Gospel is not a late, Hellenistically shaped, "Platonic" Gospel, as some critics of the 19th century supposed, but in many ways, just as "Jewish" as Matthew's Gospel.

    1. Archaeology has tended to confirm the Gospel's accuracy concerning Palestine, and it is a reliable source for relations with Samaritans and Jewish messianic expectations.

    2. The religious and ethical dualism that earlier scholars considered Greek is found in much the same form in the Dead Sea Scrolls from Qumran, another sectarian Jewish group hostile to outsiders.

B. In fact, there are elements in John that can be read positively with regard to the Jewish tradition.

    1. In conversation with the Samaritan woman, Jesus declares that "salvation is from the Jews" (4:22).

    2. In the prologue, 1:17 identifies the Law as a "grace" that is fulfilled by the "grace and truth" revealed by the Son.

    3. John insists that the proper understanding of scripture is as a witness to Jesus (5:38–40).

    4. John uses the symbolism of the traditional Jewish feasts to show that Jesus is the fulfillment of all the ways that

God's presence was mediated to the people: He is Hanukkah (temple), Passover (bread and lamb), Booths (water and light).

C. But the overwhelming impression given by John's language is negative toward the Jews as a people.

    1. The Gospel may well have arisen from the actual experience of expulsion from the synagogue because of confessing Jesus as Messiah (9:22).

    2. But John's drama demands minimizing any differentiation between individual Jews or even parties within Judaism (although the Pharisees still play a role); "the Jews" simply stands for opposition to Jesus (= God).

IV. Two conversations reveal the complexity of John's portrayal of Jesus within Judaism.

    A. In conversation with Nicodemus, a Pharisee and "ruler of the Jews," Jesus reveals the distance between himself and those who are not "born from above" (3:1–15; see 19:39).

    B. After the healing of the man born blind, the conversation reveals who really sees and who is really blind (9:1–41).

Essential Reading
The Gospel of John, 3, 4, 9.

Supplementary Reading:
C. K. Barrett, *The Gospel of John and Judaism*, translated by D. M. Smith (Philadelphia: Fortress Press, 1975).

W. A. Meeks, "'Am I a Jew?' Johannine Christianity and Judaism," in *Christianity, Judaism, and Other Greco-Roman Cults*, edited by J. Neusner, pp. 163–186 (SJLA 12; Leiden: Brill, 1975).

Questions to Consider:
1. Discuss the distinct ways in which the Gospels of Matthew and John negotiate their respective contexts of conflict with formative Judaism.

2. In what ways does John seek to communicate the full humanity of Jesus?

Lecture Twenty-Three—Transcript
Gospel of John—Jesus as Obedient Son

In the last lecture, I showed some of the ways in which John shows Jesus to be the man from heaven, the one who reveals God in the world. In one way, nothing is hidden in this Gospel. Everything is out in plain sight. Jesus is called son of God by human characters from the beginning, in sharp contrast to Mark's Gospel in which only Jesus's executioner recognizes him as son of God, and at the end of John's Gospel Jesus is even called by Thomas, "My Lord and my God," thus identifying him in the highest possible fashion. Yet, oddly, Jesus also retains an air of mystery in this Gospel, not least because from another side, the one about whom all these things are being said, is also deeply human, enmeshed in the world of Judaism and the obedient son of the one who sent him. In this lecture, I want to try to put that other side of the picture into our understanding.

Let me begin with the observation that the powerful poetry of the Fourth Gospel has had a powerful effect on readers throughout history, but that effect is both positive and negative. For Christian theologians, John is the great source of doctrine concerning Jesus, especially his divine status, precisely because of the explicitness of John's propositions. "God so loved the world as to send his only son," John 3:16, appears not only on the hats of crazy people at ball games but has played a very important role in the history of Christian theology. John's Gospel is the supreme source for creedal statements within Christianity concerning Jesus as the word of God. The Nicene Creed says of Jesus that he is light from light, true light from true light, begotten, non-made, one in being with the Father. This kind of language clearly derives from the explicit character of the statements found in John's Gospel. We could not find that in the Synoptic Gospels; it is John.

For mystics throughout the history of Christianity and for ordinary readers, John's Jesus represents the deep heart of the Christian reality. Indeed, I think it is a true statement—I've tested it with a number of students—that most people who think about Jesus think about Jesus with the Synoptic plot but with a Johannine heart. They picture Jesus as doing the things that the Synoptic Gospels report him doing, but it's sort of the John Jesus who's doing them, so that they have the sense that John really gives us the true identity of Jesus, and that's an understandable and probably appropriate way of harmonizing the distinct witnesses in the Synoptics and John's Gospel.

But I think the negative effects are more subtle, and they are two. The first is that when readers fail to take into account the nature of John's Gospel as reflective and making explicit the things that are implicit in the story of Jesus, and in which therefore John's claims are taken as literal, historical, and exclusive, so that when Jesus says, "I am the way and the truth and the life; no one can come to the father except through me" in John, Chapter 14, Verse 6, this is taken not only as a literal statement of Jesus at the Last Supper rather than the reflection of the Johannine community on the identity of Jesus but is also taken as exclusively true in contrast to the statements made, for example, in Mark's Gospel about the end. "Nobody knows, not the angels in heaven, not even the son," so that John's Gospel is not only regarded as true but exclusively true.

This cultivates within some Christians, especially Johannine exclusive readers of John's Gospel, a sectarian attitude hostile to outsiders, so that if one is not explicitly Christian, then one is not truly Christian, so that the same kind of attitude that John's Gospel has about everything made explicit is found in certain Christians for whom, if you don't make certain kinds of formal verbal kinds of statements, then one is not really Christian at all, so that there is a tendency to equate the explicit with the authentic rather than the implicit as equally valid.

Above all, John's Gospel is one of the main sources for the strain of anti-Semitism that runs through Christian theology and Christian behavior throughout history. Now by no means should John be considered exclusively in this regard. Certainly there are statements in Paul's letters that can be twisted in an anti-Semitic direction. Certainly, as we saw in Matthew's Gospel, the statement in Matthew 27:25, "His blood be upon us and upon our children," is the classic text that was used by Christian anti-Semites but, nevertheless, John's

Gospel's way of making the Jews represent the unbelieving world is powerful medicine and creates a powerful impression.

What I'm getting at here, and I'll try to work this out in the course of this lecture, in the course of this lecture I will try to work this out, but, in the same way that Jesus is not a realistic figure in John but rather a representative figure, the same effect applies also to the Jews. They are not individual persons who are realistically depicted; they are rather characters in a cosmic drama, and the consequence is that they are made to play the role of the heavy, which is a difficult role to play, especially again if we forget that it's poetry and literalize it and make it an accurate descriptor of who Jews are and were with respect to Jesus.

But taking all of that as read, let me turn to the other side of the coin for a while, because in many respects John's Jesus is the most intensely human of all the Gospels; even those theologians who insisted on Jesus's divinity also insisted that when John says the word became flesh, he was serious and not just meat but real humanity, that the Jesus of John's Gospel is a real human Jesus, so it's a natural tendency to focus only on the divine dimensions of Jesus in the Fourth Gospel. Because Jesus represents God in this drama, his actions and speech almost seem to hover over the surface. He never quite touches ground, so in 8:46, the people sent to spy out Jesus in his language return and says, "No one has ever spoken like this man," and it's true. We often don't have people give revelatory monologues about how they represent the Father.

In the last lecture, we saw how Jesus's language ascribed to him by John of "I am, I am the way and the truth and the light" or simply absolutely "I am" certainly gives the impression of a divine visitor in our midst, so much so that even within the narrative John has his opponents recognize that these claims are outrageous for a human being to make. In Chapter 10, Verse 31, pages the Jews took up stones again to stone him. Jesus answered them, "I've shown you many good works from the Father. For which of these do you stone me?" The Jews answered him, "It is not for a good work that we stone you but for blasphemy because you, being a man, make yourself God." That certainly is the implication of that side of Jesus's speech and action in John's Gospel.

But as analysts of the Gospels as literary works, we need to be a bit more subtle in our approach and analyze a bit more carefully. Remember in the Gospel of Mark, the humanity of Jesus seemed to be fairly obvious, but by no means was Jesus in Mark's Gospel simply a Jewish teacher or a nice Jewish boy from down the street. We saw that Mark's Jesus was indeed a powerful and mysterious figure through whom God was at work. Similarly in the Fourth Gospel, Jesus's humanity, though subdued, is displayed in some fairly remarkable ways. Notice that it is in John's Gospel that Jesus is said to have a number of distinctive human traits that are not ascribed to him in the Synoptics.

In John's Gospel, Jesus gets tired. He has fatigue when he sits at the well when he encounters the Samaritan woman in 4:6. Jesus experiences anguish in 12:27. When Jesus is contemplating his rejection and death, he cries out, "Now is my soul troubled, and what shall I say? Father, save me from this hour? No, for this purpose I have come to this hour. Father, glorify thy name," so he experiences anguish. Again, in Chapter 13, Verse 21, when Jesus has talked about being accepted or rejected, he was troubled in spirit and testified, "Truly, truly, I say to you, one of you will betray me," so he experiences a troubledness within himself. He weeps at the death of a friend; when his friend Lazarus dies, Jesus weeps. Even, quite remarkably for somebody who represents God, in Chapter 7, Verses 1-10, Jesus changes his mind. He says "I'm not going to go to Jerusalem," and then he says, "After all, I think I am going to go to Jerusalem."

It's striking that in John's Gospel alone does Jesus actually enter into long conversations with people. In the Synoptics, we have this set tendency to have somebody confront Jesus and then Jesus deals with them with a one-liner. In John, people don't go away that easily, and so both with his friends and with his opponents Jesus enters into long conversations. Look at Chapter 4, Verses 7-26, with Jesus and the Samaritan woman in which it becomes clear at some points that the Samaritan woman is getting the best of the conversation. She's a real human being, and Jesus is a real human being; there's real interaction.

In John's Gospel, Jesus shows suspicion of others, irritation at others, and he has real friends. He calls his followers friends, and people like Lazarus and Mary and Martha really appear as friends of Jesus in this Gospel. Indeed, there's a plaintive quality to even the resurrected Lord in Chapter 21, Verses 15-17, asking Peter three times, "Simon Peter, do you love me more than these do?" and then again "Do you love me? Do you love me?" There's this need for reciprocity and for response. These are profoundly human qualities that are ascribed to Jesus. Since Jesus is talking and acting like a hovercraft above the earth, we tend to see that rather than these qualities, so it's not a realistic depiction of humanity, and yet, if we look more carefully, he really is human.

In that same way, I want to emphasize the fact that Jesus in John's Gospel is also, as human, obedient to God, so that he is not simply God. Rather, he is the son who is obedient to the father and is so precisely as a human being. This is perhaps said most explicitly in Chapter 5, Verse 19, right after Jesus heals the paralytic at the pool in Jerusalem and is challenged because he was healing on the Sabbath. Jesus said to his opponents, "Truly, truly, I say to you, the son can do nothing of his own accord, but only whatever he sees the father doing, for whatever he does, that the son does likewise," and then he goes on to talk about the various things that the father does and that the son does as well. Embedded in this is a mini-parable of the son observing his father in the workshop.

The son learns from the father how to act and what to do, and Jesus is sort of applying that same relationship of what he has seen and what he has heard from the father, that's what he himself does. He says in Verse 30, Chapter 5, "I can do nothing on my own authority. As I hear, I judge, and my judgment is just because I seek not my own will, but the will of him who sent me," so Jesus is not on his own hook; he is rather witnessing to God. If I bear witness to myself, my testimony is not true. There is another who bears witness to me, and I know that the testimony which he bears me is true, so Jesus is, as human, one who is obedient to the father who sent him. It's a side of

John's Gospel which is subtle, somewhat difficult to grasp, but I think it deserves emphasis.

Let's turn to the other side of Jesus's humanity, which is John's relationship with Judaism and Jesus's relationship to Judaism. This is similarly very complex and has positive and negative features. Let me begin by stating that John's Gospel is not, as was popularly understood by critics of the 19th century, a late Gospel composition shaped by Platonic philosophy. It was regularly dated well into the 2nd century because of the perception that John's Gospel was influenced by Greek philosophy, and the reason for this was the way in which John uses, in a manner unlike the Synoptics, abstract nouns, so truth, falsehood, light, darkness, flesh, spirit, these dualisms seemed to people who had not yet read the Qumran scrolls to be characteristic of Greek rather than Jewish thought. But in many ways, John's Gospel is just as Jewish as Matthew's Gospel is.

A couple of points on this: First, archaeology remarkably has tended to confirm the Gospels' accuracy concerning Palestine. In other words, what John reports to us about the topography, geography, and customs of Palestine tends to be as verified by archaeology as what the Synoptics say and is perhaps in some respects more accurate. For example, scholars used to scoff at the notion that there was a pool in Jerusalem with five porticos, as reported in Chapter 5, Verses 2-3, but archaeologists have confirmed the presence of such a pool. Did the water stir up from time to time and people go into that pool for healing? That, archaeologists can't confirm, but the presence of the pool is there.

Likewise, it used to be thought a legendary note in Chapter 19:13, when John refers to the *Lithostrotos*, the rocky pavement in the courtyard where Pilate judged Jesus, but archaeology has confirmed a cobbled stone floor in that place. But beyond sites, John's Gospel is reliable for Jewish relations with Samaritans, as reported in Chapter 4, where the Samaritan woman talks about the worship of God on Mount Gerizim, and that we worship God here in our temple and you Jews have your temple in Jerusalem. That relationship of temple worship, and the fact, as John said, that Jews have no dealings with Samaritans, this is accurate with regard to 1st-century Palestine.

Even, and quite unexpectedly, John gives us information about contemporary Jewish messianic expectations, which are not found in the Synoptic Gospels, so when Nathaniel says that nothing messianic can come out of Nazareth in 1:46, it clearly reflects a perception that Nazareth is not a leading candidate for the appearance of a messiah, or when the Samaritan woman says to Jesus that "When the messiah comes, he will show us all things" corresponds to a tradition that we now find in the Qumran literature that in fact there was an expectation of the messiah to be an interpreter of Torah and to reveal all the mysteries or when the people see Jesus multiply the loaves, and they said, "This is the prophet who has come into the world," in Chapter 6:14, and then John notes they wanted to make him king.

We find here a reflection of a form of Jewish messianic expectation grounded in Deuteronomy 18:15, the prophet like Moses who will also be a prophet king, and that is distinctive, for example, to Samaritan messianic expectations, and John reports that positively, or in Chapter 12, Verse 34, when the crowd says to Jesus that "We have heard from the law that the messiah will remain forever." They haven't heard it from the law, but they have heard it from contemporary Jewish expectations concerning the messiah. All of these things show a Gospel of John which is not out in the Diaspora, remote and shaped by Platonic philosophy, but deeply enmeshed in actual knowledge about the world of Palestine and thus supports at some level the fact that at root there may well be a kind of eyewitness or participant basis for John's Gospel as for the Synoptics.

In fact, this has been tremendously supported by the discovery of the Dead Sea Scrolls. One of the effects of the discovery of the Dead Sea Scrolls at Wadi Qumran in 1947 was not simply the light it threw upon sectarian movements in Judaism, which the Essenes were, but also the fact that the kind of language that John uses in Greek is found in Hebrew in these Dead Sea Scrolls, which are profoundly dualistic and profoundly sectarian. They think all other Jews are bad except themselves, and so they use the same kind of language about a spirit of falsehood out there as opposed to a spirit of truth in here, that they are in darkness, we are in light, they don't have the spirit, we have the spirit, that kind of thing, so this language of intense ethical and even cosmological dualism is perfectly possible in the Judaism of the first century.

All of these factors have helped scholars to appreciate the embeddedness of John's Gospel in contemporary Judaism. One effect is to make us see John as probably earlier in its origin than we had formerly thought but the other is to give a better understanding to the social dimensions of John's symbolism, that what we have here is something very like the Essenes who, in support of their teacher of righteousness, used this language of dualism over against the outside world. John is in the same kind of competitive relationship with other Jews; he's been kicked out of the synagogue and therefore uses this language of us versus them, which, and here's the problem, once John's language, which is utterly intelligible historically in terms of its social contents, the polemic used by rival schools within Judaism and within Hellenistic philosophies makes perfect good sense.

It's the way we talk about outsiders in order to reinforce our own identity. "We've been kicked out of the synagogue; we are the ones who really have the truth. We're the ones who really have the messiah." That's all perfectly intelligible. What happens when John's Gospel becomes part of scripture, and when John's Gospel becomes part of a canon of scripture, and John's Gospel is regarded as inspired by God and revealed truth and literally the truth, is that language whose function we can understand in its historical context now becomes dehistoricized and literalized in a way which can be very, very dangerous.

Beyond this embeddedness of John's Gospel in Judaism, there are elements in John's Gospel that can be read positively with regard to the Jewish tradition. In conversation with the Samaritan woman, John has Jesus say, "Salvation comes from the Jews," in 4:22, and even though he goes on to say that "God is spirit and God desires those who worship him in spirit and truth," so neither Mount Gerasene nor Jerusalem is of ultimate importance, nevertheless, that statement, "Salvation is from the Jews," is a powerful positive statement.

Likewise, in the prologue in 1:17, John identifies the law that was given through Moses as a gift, as a grace that is fulfilled by the grace in truth being given by the son, so the relationship between Moses and the son and Jesus is not one of replacement but one of coordination, if you will, or complementary relationship. There is truth to the law; there is beauty to the law. Indeed, in 5:38-40, John insists or has Jesus insist that the true meaning of scripture is to be found in its witness to Jesus. Jesus tells his opponents, "You search the scriptures because you think that in them you have eternal life, and yet it is them that bear witness to me; yet you refuse to come to me that you may have life."

Finally, John uses the symbolism of traditional Jewish feasts to show that Jesus is the fulfillment of all the ways that God's presence was mediated to the people of old. John places Jesus in the context of the feast of Hanukkah in Jerusalem, the rededication of the temple, and uses the language of Jesus as the temple, the temple of his body. He is the one on whom angels ascend and descend. John shows Jesus at three Passovers and uses the symbolism of the lamb. He is the lamb who bears the sin of the world. He is the lamb whose bones are not broken in the crucifixion. But he is also the one who multiplies the bread, and he is therefore not like Moses, who gave you bread in the wilderness, but he is the one who gives the bread that is really from heaven, namely, his own identity, his own flesh, and his own blood that you are to eat and drink.

The symbolism of the Feast of Booths, the feast in which people celebrated the time in the wilderness, and in the time of Jesus the Feast of Booths was celebrated with rituals connected to the pouring of water in the temple precincts and the carrying of lanterns and torches through the city, the symbols of light and of water, and so we have Jesus in Chapter 8, Verse 12, in the context of the Feast of Booths saying, "I am the light of the world," appropriating that symbolism of light to himself. Even more dramatically, we have in Chapter 7, Verse 37, "On the last day of the feast (this is the Feast of Booths), the great day, Jesus stood up and proclaimed, 'If anyone thirst, let him come to me and drink.'" Remember when he was talking to the Samaritan woman, he talked about the water that he would give would be the water for the life of the world. "Let anybody who come to me and drink, whoever believes in me, as scripture says, out of his heart shall flow rivers of living water." Remember that symbolism; I'll pick it up in the next lecture.

This he said about the spirit which those who believed in him were to receive, for as yet the spirit was not given because Jesus was not yet glorified. Again, as I said last class, this is that reflection afterward. They see that what Jesus was talking about, out of his side will come rivers of living water; this means the spirit that is going to be received. But this is the symbolism of the Jewish Feast of Booths, so that what John is trying to do is to say everything that mediated God's presence in the law—Passover, the temple, the Feast of Booths, Hanukkah—all of this stuff is found in the single figure of Jesus. He is the new source of life for the people. But, nevertheless, despite all those positive statements, the overwhelming impression given by John's language is negative toward the Jews as a people.

We can notice that John, for example, will start off in a place like 8:13 talking about the Pharisees, a specific group. But very quickly in 8:48, it's simply the Jews. People will insist that's just a geographical designation, the Judeans, but in the history of Christianity it's taken to represent the Jews as a religious people, so the Jews again in Chapter 9, Verse 13, the Pharisees become the Jews in the course of this dialogue, so the Gospel, as I've suggested, may well have arisen from the actual experience of expulsion from the synagogue because of confessing Jesus as the Messiah in 9:22, but John's drama demands minimizing any differentiation between individual Jews or even parties within Judaism. The Jews have to play the onerous role of being those who simply oppose Jesus and therefore oppose God.

We can look more carefully at two conversations that reveal the complexity of John's portrayal of Jesus within Judaism. For example, the conversation with Nicodemus in the beginning of the Gospel shows that Nicodemus the Pharisee as somebody who seems to be sincere, a ruler of the Jews who really wants to understand who Jesus is as a teacher of Israel, and yet he shows himself astonishingly imperceptive. Jesus says that a person must be born from above in order to enter into the kingdom, and Nicodemus says, "You mean a person has to crawl back into his mother's womb to be born again?"

Jesus and John are playing on the Greek adverb *ono*, which can mean again or from above.

It's ironic that some present-day Christians insist on being born again on the basis of John's Gospel, but actually they are misreading what Jesus is saying in the way that Nicodemus does. Jesus says that it's not a question of being born again, it's a question of being born from above, from God, so that people either are attuned to the spirit or they're not. But Nicodemus is not, and so he doesn't get it, so that Nicodemus, notice, in 19:39 at the death of Jesus brings 100 pounds of ointment to anoint the body of Jesus. On the surface, this looks as though it's a positive gesture, an act of kindness toward Jesus. At some level, it reveals Nicodemus's continuing obtuseness; 100 pounds of nard? That's a lot of ointment; stay dead, stay really dead.

Similarly, after the healing of the man born blind, we have a long conversation between Jesus and Jewish leaders in which Jesus says to these Pharisees who simply become "the Jews" that it is precisely their insistence that they see in which the fault lies, that they are failing to recognize the light that has come into the world because they're not really blind; rather, they are closing their eyes. They are choosing not to see. It's a deliberate darkness, and for that reason they exclude themselves from the light that Jesus brings.

Lecture Twenty-Four
Gospel of John—Witness to the Truth

Scope:

In John's Gospel, the most extensive teaching of his followers takes place after the close of Jesus's public ministry. At his last meal with "those whom he loved," Jesus performs a symbolic act of service, then instructs his disciples on continuing his witness to the truth before a hostile world. John portrays Jesus's death and resurrection in terms of the "hour" of his "being lifted up" and "glorified," all themes established earlier in the narrative and here brought to full expression.

Outline

I.   In contrast to the Synoptic Gospels, John reserves the teaching of Jesus's disciples to his final meal with them before his death (13–17).

   A. The beginning of chapter 13 pulls together themes that John had anticipated earlier in the narrative: Jesus has reached his "hour," the time of his "glorification" through being "lifted up."

   B. John has no description of a "last supper" (see chapter 6 for his discourse on the Eucharist) but describes Jesus engaging in a symbolic act of service (13:4–20)

   C. After Judas leaves the group (see the symbolism of light; 13:21–31), Jesus enters into a long discourse (including questions from his disciples).

   1. They will experience what he has experienced and must, like him, witness to the truth (15:18–27).

   2. They will be strengthened by the spirit (the paraclete), whom Jesus will send to them (14:15–31; 16:5–33).

   3. They must be united with him as a vine is with branches (15:1–8), and their moral mandate is to love one another (15:9–17).

D. Jesus's "farewell address" takes the form of an extended prayer to his father for his followers, that they be "sanctified in the truth" (17:1–26).

II. The passion account in the Fourth Gospel is distinctive for its emphasis on bearing witness to the truth.

    A. There are points of similarity and dissimilarity among John and the Synoptics.

        1. They share the same basic storyline: arrest, hearings before Jewish leaders, denial by Peter, trial before Pilate, crucifixion, burial.

        2. John has no agony in the garden or formal Sanhedrin hearing.

    B. John gives particular attention to the interaction between Jesus and Pilate.

        1. Jesus is the witness to the truth, and Pilate's authority is not absolute (18:36–38; 19:11).

        2. In an intensely ironic scene, Pilate enthrones Jesus as "king of the Jews" and is rejected by the Jews (19:13–16).

    C. The death of Jesus is interpreted through Torah, as in the Synoptics, but the emphases are distinctive.

        1. The identification of Jesus as "king of the Jews" is affirmed by Pilate (19:17–22).

        2. Jesus is accompanied by faithful women, his mother, and "the Beloved Disciple" (19:23–30).

        3. The piercing of Jesus's side points symbolically (through scriptural allusion) to the outpouring of the Spirit (see Zech. 12:10).

III. John's resurrection stories agree with the Synoptics only in their convictions but are completely different in form.

    A. John's empty-tomb story involves Mary of Magdala, Peter, and the Beloved Disciple (20:1–18).

    B. The appearance to the gathered disciples is John's "Pentecost": Jesus imparts the Holy Spirit and commissions them (20:19–22).

C. The story of doubting Thomas delivers a message to the readers of the Gospel (20:24–31).

D. The epilogue (21:1–25) presents a final appearance of Jesus to his followers (21:1–14) and answers lingering questions concerning the destiny of Peter and the Beloved Disciple (21:15–23).

Essential Reading:

The Gospel of John, 13–21.

Supplementary Reading:

F. F. Segovia, *The Farewell of the Word: The Johannine Call to Abide* (Minneapolis: Fortress Press, 1991).

Questions to Consider:

1. How does John's farewell discourse to Jesus's disciples help shape a distinctive image of Jesus as revealer?

2. According to the logic of John's narrative, what truth is it that Jesus has come to bear witness to?

Lecture Twenty-Four—Transcript
Gospel of John—Witness to the Truth

We have seen how John, the most Christocentric of Gospels, has portrayed Jesus both in his divinity, the man from heaven, and in his humanity. Now, as we move to the last part of John's Gospel, we want to pay particular attention to the followers of Jesus, those who are called to continue Jesus's own witness to the truth. I want to begin this class by looking at the end of the Book of Signs. We saw that the Book of Signs, Chapter 1-12, is really all of Jesus's miracles and the controversies that they generated. John gives a decisive turn to the end of that portion of his Gospel. He has Jesus say to the crowds, "The light is with you for a little longer. Walk while you have the light, lest the darkness overtake you. He who walks in the darkness does not know where he goes. While you have the light, believe in the light that you may become sons of the light." This is Jesus's last statement in Chapter 12, Verse 35, immediately before moving to Chapter 13.

John concludes with an interpretation of that last call. He says, "When Jesus had said this, he departed and hid himself from them," so we have this picture of the light in the world, the world not walking in the light, and then the light sort of departing from the world, and in the next scene, in Chapter 13, Jesus will be with his disciples alone. It's sort of like the diffused light has come down into this focused light; it is Jesus and his disciples as though he were the candle and they were gathered around him. The light is no longer out there available. They chose not to have it, and so it's withdrawn from them, and John at this point applies the saying of Isaiah about, although they had eyes, they didn't see, and ears, they didn't hear. They have become blinded to the light because, as I said in an earlier lecture, they preferred the glory that they received from other humans than the glory they got from God.

This is a decisive closing of the open ministry of Jesus, and in Chapter 13 Jesus turns to the teaching of his disciples in his final meal with them before his death. This is a tightly focused group around

Jesus. The beginning of Chapter 13 pulls together themes that John had anticipated earlier in his narrative. Jesus had talked earlier, for example in Chapter 2, when his mother wanted him to supply wine for the wedding, and Jesus says, "My hour is not yet here," and other places in the Gospel he talks about his hour was not yet. No, finally, when he comes to this meal with his disciples, Jesus has reached his hour, the time of his glorification through being lifted up. All of these things come together.

This is the way Chapter 13 begins, "Now before the feast of the Passover, when Jesus knew that his hour had come to depart out of this world to the Father, having loved his own who were in the world, he loved them to the end," so Jesus is the one who has come from God, and now he's going to depart from the world and return to God. It is this descent and ascent movement. Notice in Verse 3, "Jesus, knowing that the Father had given all things into his hands, and that he had come from God and was going to God, rose from supper, laid aside his garments, and girded himself with a towel." So if John's Book of Signs, the first part of John's Gospel, makes things explicit, the Book of Glory makes them even more explicit; now the language is perfectly clear. Jesus has come from God and is returning to God. Everything is laid out with crystal clarity.

As we look at Chapters 13-17, I say this is Jesus's last meal with his disciples, and it is clear that a meal has taken place. He rose from supper; but for those who have read the other Gospels, the thing that's most striking is that John gives us no Last Supper. There is no description of Jesus's last meal with his followers, which in the Synoptic Gospels involves Jesus interpreting the bread and the wine as his body and his blood—none of that here. We have to go to Chapter 6 to find that language. In Chapter 6, we saw that Jesus had multiplied the loaves in the wilderness, had walked across the water, and then he gives this long discourse to his followers about being the bread that has come down from heaven.

That revelation of himself as the bread creates controversy, and the Jews disputed among themselves (beginning in Verse 52), How can this man give us his flesh to eat? Jesus said to them, "Truly, truly, I say to you, unless you eat the flesh of the son of man and drink his blood, you have no life in you. He who eats my flesh and drinks my blood has eternal life, and I will raise him up at the last day, for my flesh is food indeed and my blood is drink indeed. He who eats my flesh and drinks my blood abides in me and I in him." This, in effect, is the language of the bread and the wine being his body and blood which the other Gospels put at the end of Jesus's ministry; here it is in his discourse in Chapter 6.

John's language is so outrageous in that passage—he uses the Greek word *trogon*, he who munches my flesh. It's not delicate, so either pagan observers of Christianity are correct and pagans are cannibals who eat people's flesh, or the language is deliberately so physical to startle us into recognizing its profoundly symbolic character. In any case, we don't have a supper here. Rather, John has Jesus perform another sacrament, if you will, and what's really striking of course in the history of Christianity is that this is the one occasion in which Jesus actually says you're supposed to do this.

"If I then, your Lord and teacher, have washed your feet, you are also to wash one another's feet. I've given you an example that you should do this." It never became one of the seven sacraments of Christianity. It is celebrated on Maundy Thursday by many Christians, the washing of feet, but this for John clearly was an extraordinarily important symbolic gesture of Jesus, washing the feet of his disciples as an act of service to them, to show that authority within this community is to be a form of service. In effect, John has provided a scene which says or shows what Luke has Jesus telling when he says, "I am among you as one who serves."

That act of service is followed by its contrary, which is the scene of the betrayal of Jesus by Judas, so we see in 13:21 Jesus is troubled in spirit and says, "One of you will betray me," and it is at this point that we find the bifurcation in the disciples. Jesus has a disciple leaning against his breast in the manner of Hellenistic meals (they are lying on their elbows, and so they can lean back into the person lying next to you) who is the disciple whom Jesus loved, which is generally taken to be the first reference to the disciple who stands at the origin of this Gospel tradition, the disciple who is John, and asks, "Who is it?" and Jesus remarkably says, "It is the one to whom I will give this morsel when I have dipped it." He dips the morsel and he gives it to Judas.

The body language here and the symbolism is just really scary. You have almost Jesus dips the bread, gives it to Judas, and after the morsel Satan enters into him, very powerful, so that they were sharing the bread and so forth among themselves. Now he is assigned to do his dirty deed, and Judas leaves, and notice the symbolism. We saw how the light was concentrated with Jesus and his disciples. "After receiving the morsel, he immediately went out and it was night," so we have Judas going out of the circle of light into the darkness, where he belongs as a betrayer of the light. After that has been done, after the light has become purely concentrated around Jesus, Jesus enters into a long discourse.

There are several features of this discourse which I want to note. One of them is: you will notice that in 13:36 Simon Peter says to him, "Lord, where are you going?" In 14:4, Thomas said, "Lord, we do not know where you are going. How can we know the way?" In 14:8, Philip says to him, "Lord, show us the father and we will be satisfied." In 14:22, Judas (and the author helpfully says not Iscariot) said to him, "Lord, how is it that you will manifest yourself to us and not to the world?" and then finally in 16:29, all his disciples say, "Now you are speaking plainly, not from any figure." What I'm pointing to here is the dialogical form of the discourse here. We have disciples setting up the discourse by asking questions of Jesus. Why this is important is that various Gnostic gospels will pick up this literary technique and make it even more prominent, in which we have questions put to Jesus by his followers, and we see that literary form here already in the Gospel of John.

That's in terms of form; in terms of content, there are several themes that are struck here that are very important. The first is that Jesus makes manifest to them, explicit to them, that they, his followers, will experience what he has experienced and must therefore be like him, witnesses to the truth. Notice in Chapter 15:18-27, the language is stark. "If the world hates you, know that it has hated me before it hated you." You see the very strong sectarian character of this language. "If you were of the world, the world would love its own;

but because you are not of the world, but I chose you out of the world, therefore the world hates you." I've talked about the sort of merging of horizons of the story of Jesus and the experience of the Johannine community. Here once more we see this. They are experiencing hatred from the world, meaning "the synagogue down the street" just as Jesus experienced the hatred of the world. Why?

He continues, "Remember the word that I said to you, `A servant is not greater than his master.' If they persecuted me, they will persecute you; if they kept my word, they will keep yours also. But all this they will do to you on my account, because (and here's the key) they do not know the one who sent me," so that in John, if you didn't get Jesus, you don't get God. "If I had not come and spoken to them, they would not have sin, but now they have no excuse in their sin." He continues, "It's not just the one who hates you hates me; the one who hates me hates my father also. This is the way John lines up these equations; it's all terribly explicit. This is what they are going to experience.

Second, in that experience of persecution and hatred from the side of the world, they are going to be strengthened by a new form of presence of Jesus. John here uses the language of the spirit, whom he calls the Paraclete. The term paracletus in Greek means quite literally an advocate, like a lawyer. It is sometimes called the consoler, and that is also a possibility, but this is the spirit who Jesus will send to them and will strengthen them and enlighten them as they face their uncertain future. We can look at 14:15-31, where this language of the counselor runs through this section. "If you love me, you will keep my commandments. And I will pray to the Father, and he will give you another Counselor, to be with you for ever, even the Spirit of truth, whom the world cannot receive, because it neither sees him nor knows him; you know him, for he dwells in you, and will be in you."

What John is showing us here is a dimension of this sectarian self-consciousness. Just as Jesus and the world were at odds, the spirit of Jesus is now in them and so they are in the same position as Jesus was. They have the truth inside of them; the world doesn't. Again, 14:25, "These things I have spoken to you, while I am still with you.

But the Counselor, the Holy Spirit, whom the Father will send in my name, he will teach you all things, and bring to your remembrance all that I have said to you." This is that text that shows us how John's Gospel reads everything in the story of Jesus through the perspective of the deeper wisdom and knowledge that is given by the Paraclete. Again, in Chapter 16, Verse 5, following:

4: "I did not say these things to you from the beginning, because I was with you. (Jesus's presence was with them)

5: But now I am going to the one who sent me; yet none of you asks me, 'Where are you going?'

6: But because I have said these things to you, sorrow has filled your hearts.

7: Nevertheless I tell you the truth: it is to your advantage that I go away, for if I do not go away, the Counselor will not come to you; but if I go, I will send him to you.

8: And when he comes, he will convince the world concerning sin and righteousness and judgment:

He's like a good lawyer; he's going to convince people about "sin, because they do not believe in me; concerning righteousness, I'm going to the Father; concerning judgment, because the ruler of this world is judged." Jesus says, " I still have many things to say to you but you can't hear them now. When the spirit of truth comes he will guide you into all truth." Their experience will be like that of Jesus, but they will be strengthened in that experience because they will have the spirit that Jesus will send to be with them as they face it.

The third point that Jesus makes in this discourse then is that they must be united with him and with each other. Theirs is an organic living relationship, and here is where he uses the language of the vine and the branches in Chapter 15:1-8. "I am the true vine, and my Father is the vinedresser. Every branch of mine that bears no fruit, he takes away, and every branch that does bear fruit he prunes. You are already made clean by the word I have spoken to you. Abide in me, and I in you. I am the vine; you are the branches. The one who abides in me, and I in him, it is he that bears much fruit, for apart from me you can do nothing." It's extraordinary language that the spirit that is going to be among them when Jesus leaves is going to put them in an organic relationship of branches in a living tree, so that their life and their power and their effectiveness is entirely conditioned upon being, if you will, grafted into Jesus.

Then if they are grafted into him, then they will bear fruit. What is the fruit? Quite remarkable in John's Gospel, the only moral demand made upon followers, the only instruction in Christian life is a single commandment, and that is the commandment to love one another, so that John has this utterly simple religious framework of faith in Jesus as the one whom God has sent and love of other people who have that same faith. It's not a love of the world; it's a love for each other. The first letter of John will develop this in its moral dimensions more fully about the sharing of possessions and so forth, but I point this out to you because it is startling, especially when we've just been looking at the Gospel of Luke, and Luke's prophetic program, which has so much to do with the uses of power and the uses of possessions and prayer and so forth as a kind of range of moral responses that fit within the prophetic program. In John, it's much, much simpler.

In 15:12, "This is my commandment, that you love one another," but notice the kicker, "as I have loved you. Greater love has no man than this, that a man lay down his life for his friends. You are my friends if you do what I command you. No longer do I call you servants, for the servant does not know what his master is doing; but I have called you friends." This I command you, to love one another, so it's utterly simple and transparent. All they're obliged to do is hang together like branches on the vine.

This farewell discourse concludes with the long prayer of Jesus to God, Chapter 17, "When Jesus had spoken these words, he lifted up his eyes to heaven and said, 'Father, the hour has come; glorify thy Son that the Son may glorify thee.'" If the ministry of Jesus made things explicit and the farewell discourse of Jesus made things more explicit, this final prayer of Jesus to his father brings everything to a point which is utterly clear. He says to God, "When I was with them, I kept them in thy name, which thou gave me. I've guarded them, I haven't lost any of them, but now I'm coming to thee, and these things I speak in the world that they may have my joy fulfilled in themselves," so these last moments that Jesus spends with his followers are filled with the symbolism of mutuality, of mutual service, of washing each other's feet, of being united with Jesus and of loving one another and being one with Jesus and with the God who sent him, as Jesus was unified with the father.

We turn then to the passion account in John's Gospel, and it is distinctive for its emphasis on bearing witness to the truth, so that how Jesus acts in the end is going to be the model of how his followers are to be witnesses to the truth. There are points of similarity and dissimilarity among John and the Synoptics with the passion account. They clearly share the same basic story line. Jesus is arrested; there are hearings before Jewish leaders; there is the denial by Peter; there is the trial before Pilate, crucifixion, and burial. I should mention here that in the last lecture I talked about Nicodemus bringing 100 pounds of nard at the burial of Jesus. I need to correct myself. It was actually 100 pounds of myrrh and aloes that he brought, but nevertheless it was 100 pounds of ointment, and my main point about Nicodemus, I think, is clear that he's still a little confused about who Jesus is.

John has all those similarities to the Synoptic passion account, but John does not have Jesus in agony in the garden, or prayer; he does not have a formal trial with the Sanhedrin, only a hearing before Caiaphas and Annas. What gives John's passion account its particular character is the interaction between Jesus and Pilate. Jesus appears before Pilate as the witness to the truth, and Pilate's authority is not regarded as absolute. Let's look at 18:36-38, where Jesus enters into Pilate's presence. "Pilate entered the praetorium again and called Jesus and said to him, 'Are you the King of the Jews?' Jesus answered, 'Do you say this of your own accord, or did others say it to you about me?' Pilate answered, 'Am I a Jew? Your own nation and the chief priests have handed you over to me; what have you done?' Jesus answered, 'My kingship is not of this world; if my kingship were of this world, my servants would fight, that I might not be handed over to the Jews; but my kingship is not of the world.'"

Notice this language. It's Pilate who's going to execute him, but John's tendency to blame the Jews is found even in this statement that I not be handed over to the Jews. It's Pilate he's been handed over to. "Pilate answered him, 'So you are a king?' Jesus answered, 'You say that I am a king. For this I was born, and for this I have come into the world, to bear witness to the truth.'" That's how he defines his kingship. "Everyone who is of the truth hears my voice," and Pilate notoriously says, "What is truth?" this being the cynical politician who again doesn't get it, so it's not just the Jews that don't get it; it's also Pilate who doesn't get it in John's Gospel.

Then in Chapter 19, Verses 10-11, Pilate says to him, "Do you not speak to me? Do you not know that I have power to release you and power to crucify you?" Jesus answered him "You would have no power over me unless it had been given to you from above; therefore, he who delivered me to you has the greater sin," so Judas and the Jews are more responsible than Pilate. He has simply a role to play. Pilate's authority is not absolute, and Jesus's kingship is to be witness to the truth.

But there is this intensely ironic scene in 19:13-16, which is found only in John's Gospel. "Upon this, Pilate sought to release him, but the Jews cried out, 'If you release this man, you are not Caesar's friend; every one who makes himself a king sets himself against Caesar.' When Pilate heard these words, he brought Jesus out and sat him on the judgment seat at a place called the Pavement, and in Hebrew, Gab'ba-tha. Now it was the day of reparation for the Passover; it was about the sixth hour." So Pilate brings him out and sits him on the chair which represents the king's authority.

"He said to the Jews, 'Behold your King!' They cried out, 'Away with him, away with him, crucify him!' Pilate raises the ante, 'Shall I crucify your King?' The chief priests answered, 'We have no king but Caesar.' Then he handed him over to them to be crucified." It is a scene of intense irony in which Pilate does not understand what he's doing but playing the political game; the Jews are made to understand perfectly well what they're doing, but at a deeper level they don't realize what they're doing when they say, "We have no King but Caesar." In effect, they're saying, "We don't have God as our King, and we don't have the one who witnesses to the truth as our King."

We turn to the death of Jesus we find that, like the Synoptics, John interprets Jesus's death through Torah, but the emphases are distinctive. Pilate affirms Jesus's identity as King of the Jews, Jesus is accompanied by faithful women, his mother, and the beloved disciple who stand under the cross in Jesus's presence, and Jesus hands over his mother to the beloved disciple for her safekeeping. The piercing of Jesus's side after his death, which is distinctive to John's version, is interpreted symbolically as the outpouring of the spirit. This is in 19:34, "But one of the soldiers pierced his side with a spear, and at once there came out blood and water. He who saw it bore witness and his testimony is true, and he knows that he tells the truth, that you also may believe. For these things took place that the scripture might be fulfilled, 'Not a bone of him shall be broken.'" And again another scripture says, "They shall look on him whom they have pierced."

"Not a limb shall be broken." That's a line about the Pascal lamb. Jesus is the lamb of the world. They look upon him whom they have pierced as a more obscure reference, but it is to the prophet Zechariah, Chapter 12, Verse 10, "And I will pour out on the house of David and the inhabitants of Jerusalem a spirit of compassion and supplication, so that when they look on him whom they have pierced they shall mourn for him as one mourns for an only child." Here is the symbolism of the spirit coming out of the side of Jesus that we saw in Chapter 7, Verses 36-38, that the spear in Jesus's side, blood and water comes out, and John quotes a passage of scripture that interprets that as the spirit that God is going to pour out on humanity because they kill the one who is God's only son, so the scripture is used to interpret Jesus's death, although differently.

When we turn to John's resurrection stories, we see that they agree with the Synoptics only in their convictions, but they are completely different in form. We saw that John's empty tomb account involves Mary of Magdela, Peter, and the beloved disciple, and then there's a separate appearance to Mary Magdalene. The appearance of the gathered disciples is John's Pentecost, where John has Jesus say,

"Receive the spirit; whose sins you shall forgive, they are forgiven," so that this is, in effect, the giving of the spirit, the Paraclete, to these followers of Jesus after his resurrection. Then the famous story of doubting Thomas, which delivers a powerful message to the readers of the Gospel that Thomas believed because he saw, and the Gospel writer says, "Blessed are those who have not seen and who believe."

And then finally, the epilogue, which gives a final appearance of Jesus to his followers and answers lingering questions concerning the destiny of Peter—he will be bound and killed as Jesus was—and the beloved disciple, whom many of his followers seem to think that would be alive until Jesus should return. The epilogue makes clear that the beloved disciple also will experience death before the return of Jesus.

Timeline

B.C.E. (before the common era)

323............................ Death of Alexander the Great

168............................ Roman domination of the Mediterranean

168............................ War of Maccabees against Antiochus IV Epiphanes

167............................ Book of Daniel

63 .... Conquest of Palestine by Pompey

30 .... Augustus becomes Roman emperor

6................................ Judaea annexed as province by Rome

4................................ Birth of Jesus (probable)

C.E. (common era)

28 .... Ministry of John the Baptist

30 .... Crucifixion of Jesus (probable)

34/37.......................... Conversion of Saul/Paul (probable)

49–64.......................... Active ministry and letters of Paul; period of oral transmission of the memory of Jesus; formation of Q?

50 .... Activity of Apollonius of Tyana (approximate); death of Philo Judaeus

64 .... Nero burns Rome; punishes Christians

66 .... Start of Jewish War against Rome

68 .... Death of Paul (and probably Peter)

70 .... Destruction of Jerusalem Temple by Romans; probable composition of the Gospel of Mark

85 .... The Birkat ha Minim (possible); composition of the Gospel of Matthew and Luke-Acts.

90 .... Gospel of John (probable)

95 .... First Letter of Clement

100.............................. The *Didache* (probable)

107.............................. Martyrdom of Ignatius of Antioch

122–135 .... Final Jewish Revolt against Rome

135.............................. Destruction of Jerusalem by Romans; Justin's *Dialogue with Trypho* (?)

135/136 .... Valentinus in Rome; Gospel of Truth (?)

150.............................. Infancy Gospels of Thomas and James (probable); Greek original of the Sayings Gospel of Thomas (?)

155.............................. Martyrdom of Polycarp

156–170 .... Ministry of Montanus (approximate)

160.............................. Death of Marcion of Sinope; composition of the Gospel of Peter (?)

165.............................. Martyrdom of Justin

200.............................. Death of Irenaeus of Lyons; publication of the Mishnah under Judah the Prince

215.............................. Death of Clement of Alexandria

218.............................. Philostratus writes *Life of Apollonius of Tyana*

225.............................. Death of Tertullian

250.............................. Composition of Gospel (Questions) of Bartholomew (?)

254.............................. Death of Origen

313.............................. Edict of Milan

325.............................. Council of Nicaea

367.............................. Pachal Letter of Athanasius of Alexandria

397.............................. Council of Carthage

500–700 .... Composition of further apocryphal Gospels

1773 .... Discovery of manuscript of Pistis Sophia

1783 .... *Gospel Parallels* published by J. J. Griesbach

1906 .... Publication of Schweitzer's *Quest of the Historical Jesus*

1945–1946 .... Discovery of Gnostic codices at Nag Hammadi in Egypt

1947 .... Discovery of Dead Sea Scrolls at Wadi Qumran in Israel

1985 .... Formation of the Jesus Seminar

Glossary

Acts of the Apostles (also Acts): The second volume of the Gospel of Luke, therefore, of "Luke-Acts." It provides a narrative account of Christianity's first geographical expansion, with a concentration on Peter and Paul.

Apocalyptic: A vision of history as tending toward a (divinely ordered) goal, often in two stages: A present age of oppression is to be followed by an age of triumph for the righteous (also: messianic age/resurrection of the just). The term is also attached to the literature containing such views.

Apocryphal: Either Jewish or Christian literature that was not included in canonical collections; not to be used for official functions but may be read for private edification or entertainment.

Apostle: From the Greek for "one sent out on a commission," the term used in earliest Christianity for representatives of the risen Christ.

Baptism: The Christian ritual of initiation, carried out in public (probably) by means of immersion in water.

Bridal chamber: A term used in compositions from Nag Hammadi, most notably the Gospel of Philip. It appears to refer to a ritual act, but its precise meaning is uncertain.

Canon: The official collection of literature defining a religious tradition, regarded as authoritative and often as divinely inspired.

Canonical: Writings included in the collection of compositions that make up the Old and New Testaments   scripture.

Chrism: The Greek term means "anointing"; the term is used in the Gospel of Philip for one of the sacraments (confirmation?).

Christ/Christianity: The Hebrew term *Messiah* is translated into Greek as *Christos* ("anointed one"); Christianity is the religion in which Jesus the Christ is the central figure.

Circumcision: The Jewish initiation of males through removal of the foreskin of the penis, symbolizing acceptance of the obligation to observe Torah.

Cognitive dissonance: The condition in which there is a clash between an experience and a conviction (idea/symbol) or between two contradictory ideas.

Coptic: The Egyptian language written in Greek and demotic characters, used from the early Christian era; the language of the Nag Hammadi compositions.

Covenant: A binding treaty between two parties. In the biblical tradition, such treaties set out the terms of the relationship between the one God and the chosen people.

Diaspora: From the Greek, meaning "dispersion." Any place Jews live outside of Palestine. In the 1st century, more Jews lived in the diaspora than in the land of Israel.

Didache: Short title for *The Teaching* [*Didache*] *of the Twelve Apostles*, an anonymous Christian writing, c. 100.

Disciple/Discipleship: This term translates the Greek *mathetes*, which means literally "a learner"; used for followers of Jesus in the Gospels.

Docetism: From the Greek *dokein* ("to appear," "to seem"), the position that the humanity of Jesus was not real but only apparent.

Doctrine: The statement of authoritative teaching in a religious tradition, especially concerning matters of belief.

Doxa: A Greek noun that can mean "opinion" (as opposed to truth) but is used also to translate *Kbd*, thus, "glory."

Ebionites: The name derives from the Hebrew word for "poor"; a group of Jewish Christians whose origins are legendarily connected to the original Jerusalem community.

Ekklesia: The Greek word for assembly or gathering that is used both by Jews and Christians in the diaspora but becomes the distinctive Christian self-designation of "church."

Eschatology: Any understanding of the "end" of history; the term derives from the Greek *eschatos*, which means "last" or "end."

Essenes: One of the sects of Judaism in 1st-century Palestine. Some members lived at Qumran, while others lived elsewhere. They were dedicated to a strict observance of Torah, especially in matters of purity.

Eucharist: From the Greek word for "thanksgiving," the term used for the fellowship meals celebrated in the name of Jesus among early Christians.

Formative Judaism (also Classical Judaism, Rabbinic Judaism, Talmudic Judaism): The tradition of the Pharisees with the technical expertise of the Scribes that came to dominate Judaism after the fall of the temple in diaspora synagogues.

Formgeschichte: The German designation for "form criticism."

Gentile: The term can be used equally for the "nations" other than Israel and for individuals who are not Jewish.

Glossolalia: One of the spiritual gifts in early Christianity, consisting of an ordered form of babbling; "speaking in tongues."

Gnosticism/Gnostic: Terms used to designate groups from the 2nd century onward who claimed the name of Christian and understood it as a religion of enlightenment through saving knowledge.

Gospel: The term used for the Greek *euangelion* ("good news"), which in the beginning of Christianity, referred to the proclamation of God's work in the death and resurrection of Jesus and later was used for a variety of literary works involving Jesus.

Greco-Roman: The cultural mix of the 1st-century Mediterranean world, in which Greek civilization continued to exercise influence under Roman political rule.

Hellenism: The cultural reality that resulted from Alexander the Great's effort to universalize the classical Greek culture of Athens.

Hermetic literature: Works on revelation associated with Hermes; written in Greek and Latin in the 1st–3rd centuries C.E.

Jewish-Christian: A catchall term for any followers of Jesus who are not only ethnically Jewish (and practice circumcision) but who continue to have an allegiance to the observance of Torah, however understood.

Lord's Supper: See **Eucharist**.

Magic: From one perspective, a term used to deprecate a religion not one's own. From another perspective, a relationship to transcendent power that is fundamentally manipulative.

Mantic prophecy: A much-respected form of prophecy in Hellenism, because of the conviction that the divine spirit (*pneuma*) spoke through humans in a state called *enthusiasmos*, or *mania*.

Merkabah mysticism: A form of Jewish mysticism in which the heavenly "throne chariot" is the central symbol and involves the "ascent" to the divine presence. Closely aligned with apocalyptic visions. It is found in Hekaloth ("heavenly throne room") literature.

Midrash: The practice of the interpretation of Torah among Jewish scholars (Scribes), in which ancient texts were contemporized. If legal texts are interpreted, it is *halachic* midrash; if non-legal, it is *haggadic* midrash.

Mishnah: The authoritative collection of Jewish law derived from Torah through midrash, compiled by Judah the Prince c. 200 C.E.

Monotheism: A belief distinctive to Judaism in antiquity—although some philosophers floundered toward it—that God was singular in existence, the one power that creates, sustains, and judges the world.

Mysticism: The element in a religion by which an individual seeks an unmediated experience of the divine through prayer or some other practice.

Paraclete: The Greek *parakletos* ("advocate") is used by the Fourth Gospel for the Holy Spirit.

Parousia: Literally "arrived," used for visits of royalty and, in the New Testament, for the "second coming" of Jesus.

Patristic: From the Greek for "father," the designation for Christian literature (above all, orthodox Christian literature) from the time of the New Testament to the medieval period.

Pharisee/Pharisaism: One of the sects of Judaism in f^t-century Palestine, notable for its deep devotion to Torah and destined to become the main surviving rival to Christianity after the destruction of the temple. See also **Formative Judaism.**

Pleroma: From the Greek word for "fullness," the complex inner world of the divine in some Gnostic speculation. Detachment from the pleroma is the first disaster leading to the formation of the material world.

Polytheism: The religious system that thinks of the divine power as distributed among many gods and goddesses, often envisaged in terms of an extended family (for example, the Olympians).

Proselytes: In Greek, "those who have come over," namely, converts to Judaism from among Gentiles.

Pseudo-Clementine literature: A complex body of writings all associated (pseudonymously) with Clement of Rome. Composed between the 3rd and 4th centuries C.E., they may contain some earlier traditions. As a whole, they exhibit a Jewish-Christian tendency.

Quelle: Conventionally, the designation Q for the hypothetical shared source of Matthew and Luke comes from this German word meaning "source."

Sadducees: One of the 1st-century Jewish sects in Palestine, closely associated with the temple and the high-priestly aristocracy.

Septuagint (also LXX): The translation of the Torah into Greek carried out in Alexandria, c. 250 B.C.E.; the name comes from the tradition that 70 translators were involved.

Son of Man: The self-designation of Jesus in all four canonical Gospels. The Greek *hvios tou anthropou* is a wooden translation of a Hebrew or Aramaic original.

Sophia: The Greek word for "wisdom," which in some Gnostic literature is personified as an element in the Pleroma and as a consort of Christ.

Symbolic world: Social structures and the symbols used to express and support such structures; roughly equivalent to "culture."

Syncretism: The merging of religious traditions, specifically the fusion of polytheistic systems.

Synoptic Gospels: The Gospels of Matthew, Mark, and Luke, so called because they can be seen together (syn-opsis) when laid out in parallel columns. The complex ways in which these narratives agree and differ demands a solution of the *synoptic problem* that involves literary dependence.

Talmud: The final authoritative collection of Rabbinic lore, found in a Palestinian and Babylonian version, each completed before the 6th century C.E.

Tanak: The Jewish name for scripture, an acronym constructed from the three constitutive parts: **T**orah (the law of Moses), **N**ebiim (the prophets), and **K**etubim (the writings).

Theodicy: A defense of God's providence.

Torah: The central symbol of the Pharisaic tradition and Formative Judaism. In the narrowest sense, the five books of Moses; in a broader sense, all of scripture; in the broadest sense, all the lore and life derived from those texts.

Zealots: The Jewish sect in 1st-century Palestine that most strongly identified with the symbol of kingship and sought actively to overthrow Roman occupation.

Biographical Notes

Anna: According to the *Protevangelium Jacobi*, the mother of Mary and, therefore, the grandmother of Jesus.

Bartholomew: One of the more anonymous among the 12 disciples chosen by Jesus and, therefore, an ideal candidate to have an apocryphal work attributed to him: the Gospel (Questions) of Bartholomew.

Clement of Alexandria (c. 150–217): Head of the catechetical school at Alexandria, prolific author, and important source for our knowledge of early Gnostics, as well as Jewish-Christian Gospels, especially in his *Stromateis*.

Clement of Rome (c. 96): An elder of the church in Rome and author of a letter to the church at Corinth; one of our early sources of knowledge about the process of canonization.

Elizabeth: According to the Gospel of Luke, the mother of John the Baptist and kinswoman of Mary, the mother of Jesus.

Heracleon: A 2nd-century Gnostic teacher and an important interpreter of the Gospel of John, quoted extensively by Origen in his *Commentary on John*.

Herod: Four members of this Idumaean family who served as kings under Roman authority enter the Gospel accounts: Herod the Great was appointed king of the Jews and ruled from 37 B.C.E. to 4 B.C.E.; he is the Herod of Matt. 2:16. Herod Antipas, his son (4 B.C.E.–39 C.E.), is Herod the Tetrarch who ruled in Galilee (Luke 3:1) and beheaded John the Baptist. Agrippa I is the Herod who kills James in Acts 12:1 and himself dies a terrible death; he is the nephew of Antipas and ruled from 37–44 C.E. Finally, his son, Agrippa II, is King Agrippa, before whom Paul appears on trial in Acts 25:13.

Ignatius of Antioch (c. 35–107): The seven letters he wrote to churches while crossing Asia Minor as a prisoner on his way to being martyred at Rome are important sources for knowledge of Christianity in the early 2nd century, especially as battling Jewish

Christian manifestations on one side and Docetic elements on the other.

Irenaeus of Lyons (130–200 C.E.): His five-book treatise, *Against Heresies*, is a leading source of knowledge concerning Gnosticism, especially of the Valentinian type. The entire first book is taken up with a description of the Gnostic system.

James: There are many figures with this name in the New Testament. The most significant is the "Brother of the Lord" (so called by Paul), who was head of the church in Jerusalem after Peter (see Acts 15) and who may have written the New Testament Letter of James. The Infancy Gospel of James is certainly not by him. In the 3rd century, James of Jerusalem is a hero in some portions of the pseudo-Clementine literature, which is also hostile to the apostle Paul.

Jesus of Nazareth (c.4 B.C.E.–30 C.E.): The figure on whom all the Gospel literature centers was a Jew from Nazareth in Galilee who exercised a prophetic ministry among his fellow Jews, gained a following for his teaching and wonderworking, met opposition from religious and political leaders, and was executed by Roman authority. After his death, his followers proclaimed him as Lord and spread the "good news" of his powerful presence among them.

Joachim: According to the *Protevangelium Jacobi*, the father of Mary and, therefore, the grandfather of Jesus.

John the Baptist: A figure of 1st-century Palestine sufficiently significant to be described in his ministry and death by the historian Josephus. According to the Gospel of Luke, a cousin of Jesus, son of Zechariah and Elizabeth, and member of a priestly family from the hill country of Galilee, who proclaimed a coming kingdom of God and a baptism of repentance from sins. The Gospels portray him as the forerunner of the Messiah, the "Elijah" prophesied by Malachi. He was beheaded by Herod the Tetrarch, possibly in 28–29 C.E.

John the Evangelist: Nothing is known about the author of the Fourth Gospel, but he is associated with the "Beloved Disciple" of that narrative, the "Elder" who is the writer of 1 and 2 John, and the "Seer" of the Book of Revelation.

Joseph: The human father of Jesus (Luke says, "as it was thought"). In the Gospel of Luke, Joseph accompanies and supports Mary, but she is the hero of that account. In Matthew, Joseph emerges as the "Son of David" to whom God's plan is revealed and who acts to save the child. Given that the Gospels do not mention Joseph after the account in Luke concerning the loss of the child in the temple, he may have died before Jesus began his ministry. It is only in the Infancy Gospel of James that Joseph appears as an older man with children who takes Mary as his wife/ward; in the Infancy Gospel of Thomas, he appears as a befuddled and frightened stepfather.

Justin (c. 100–165): One of Christianity's first and greatest apologists, an opponent of the heretic Marcion. His *Dialogue with Trypho* is our best source for Jewish-Christian conditions in the mid-2nd century, and Justin's *Apology* shows knowledge of Gnostic teachers.

Lazarus: One of the few named characters in the Gospels, according to the Gospel of John, the brother of Martha and Mary, friends of Jesus. Jesus raised him from the tomb (John 11).

Luke the Evangelist: According to tradition, a companion of Paul and a physician. He may well have been a companion of Paul, who is a hero of Acts, but apart from the two-volume work (Luke-Acts) ascribed to him, we really know nothing more about him.

Marcion of Sinope (d. 160): An influential 2nd-century teacher with a sharply dualistic view: Materiality is evil, spirit is good, and Jesus delivers humans from the creator God of the Old Testament. These views resemble Gnosticism, but the exact relationship is uncertain. Marcion influenced the development of the canon by his efforts to reduce the traditional collection.

Mark the Evangelist: Nothing is known of the creator of the gospel genre, but according to Papias (a not very reliable 2nd-century writer), Mark drew his Gospel from the preaching of Peter in Rome. Present-day scholars see him as a writer of considerable artistry, despite his inelegant Greek.

Martha: With her sister Mary, she appears in both the Gospel of Luke and the Gospel of John as a friend of Jesus.

Mary, the Mother of Jesus: In the Gospels of Matthew and Luke, she appears in the infancy accounts—in Luke, she is the main figure—as Jesus's mother. In both the Synoptics and John, she appears among the followers of Jesus. In John, she is with Jesus at the cross. In Acts, she is among those who receive the Holy Spirit at Pentecost. In the *Protevangelium Jacobi*, the entire focus is on Mary and her purity, and in the Infancy Gospel of Pseudo-Matthew, Mary and Jesus have a relationship that tends to exclude Joseph.

Mary Magdalen (of Magdala): Tradition has assimilated this important witness of the resurrection to the figures of Mary (the friend of Jesus) and Luke's sinful woman. But in both John and the Synoptics, it is her role as witness to the resurrection that is most significant. In some Gnostic writings, Mary plays a role superior to that of some male disciples (see the Gospel of Mary), and some suggest a level of physical and spiritual intimacy between Jesus and Mary (see the Gospel of Philip).

Matthew the Evangelist: There is a Matthew among the 12 disciples chosen by Jesus, and those who favor this Gospel as the first written see it as an eyewitness account. But like the other Gospels, Matthew shows the signs of slow development of tradition and careful redaction of earlier sources.

Nicodemus: One of the named characters in the Fourth Gospel, the one who "comes to Jesus by night," (ch. 3) and brings ointment for his burial (ch. 19). A late apocryphal work is called the Gospel of Nicodemus.

Origen of Alexandria (184–254 C.E.): The successor to Clement in the Alexandrian catechetical school and one of the greatest theologians and interpreters of scripture in the history of Christianity, influencing all who followed. Despite sharing, with Clement, a strongly intellectual approach to the faith, he constantly repudiated the teachings of the Gnostics and adhered to the Rule of Faith handed down by tradition.

Paul (d. c. 64 C.E.): Born Saul of Tarsus in Cilicia, according to Acts, Paul was a Roman citizen by birth and a student of Gamaliel in Jerusalem. First a persecutor of the Christian movement, he encountered the risen Jesus (c. 34/37) and became an apostle, establishing churches throughout Asia Minor and Greece. He has 13 letters ascribed to him in the New Testament. He was martyred under Nero, c. 64.

Peter (d. c. 64 C.E.): According to all the Gospels, the chief spokesperson among Jesus's chosen followers and, according to Acts, the leader of the first church in Jerusalem and the first to convert a Gentile. Among a number of other apocryphal works associated with him is the Gospel of Peter.

Philip: One of the 12, who appears as an especially prominent disciple of Jesus in the Fourth Gospel, one of those who question Jesus at the last supper. He has an apocryphal gospel, the Gospel of Philip, ascribed to him.

Polycarp (c. 69–155): Bishop of Smyrna to whom Ignatius of Antioch wrote in his journey across Asia Minor and himself the author of a pastoral letter. He apparently knew and condemned Marcion and died as a martyr.

Pontius Pilate: The Roman prefect of Judaea from 26–36 C.E., under whom Jesus was crucified. The hearing before him is a climax in all the passion accounts but is expanded particularly in Matthew (where Pilate's wife makes an appearance) and in John (where Jesus and Pilate have an extended exchange). He is the classic candidate for "filling the gaps" in the narrative through apocryphal works, and an entire *Pilate cycle* of writings is extant.

Ptolemy: Gnostic teacher of the 2nd century whose *Letter to Flora* is our earliest example of a serious hermeneutical theory regarding the Christian interpretation of scripture.

Tertullian (160–225): A great apologist for Christianity and opponent of heretics, especially Marcion, for whom he is our most important source, this rigorist North African eventually joined the Montanist movement.

Thomas: One of the 12 disciples chosen by Jesus who emerges as a singular character in the Fourth Gospel, whose doubt occasioned a separate resurrection appearance. A number of apocryphal works are associated with him, including the Infancy Gospel of Thomas and the Coptic Gospel of Thomas.

Valentinus: A 2nd-century Gnostic teacher who taught at Rome from 136–165 and had hopes of being elected bishop. Passed over for that position, he seceded from the church and probably ended up in Cyprus. Possibly the author of the Gospel of Truth, Valentinus had many significant disciples, including Theodotus, Ptolemy, and Haracleon. It is his mythic system that Irenaeus reports in the first book of *Against Heresies*.

Zechariah: According to the Gospel of Luke, a member of the priestly order of Abijah and the father of John the Baptist.

Bibliography

Essential Reading:

The four canonical Gospels are conveniently available in any version of the Bible. I prefer the Revised Standard Version translation, which can be found with helpful introductions and notes in *The New Oxford Annotated Bible with the Apocrypha*, edited by H. G. May and B. M. Metzger (New York: Oxford University Press, 1973). The apocryphal Gospels are available in a number of collections. Unfortunately, all of them are seldom present in a single collection. Responsible editions include J. K. Elliott, *The Apocryphal New Testament* (Oxford: Clarendon Press, 1993); E. Hennecke, *New Testament Apocrypha*, edited by W. Schneemelcher (Philadelphia: Westminster Press, 1963), Vol. 1: *Gospels and Related Writings*; J. M. Robinson (ed.), *The Nag Hammadi Library in English* (New York: Harper and Row, 1977); B. Layton, *The Gnostic Scriptures* (New York: Doubleday, 1987); B. D. Ehrman, *Lost Scriptures: Books That Did Not Make It into the New Testament* (New York: Oxford University Press, 2003); R. J. Miller, *The Complete Gospels* (Sonoma, CA: Polebridge Press, 1992); and W. Barnstone (ed.), *The Other Bible* (San Francisco: Harper and Row, 1982). For comparison to Greco-Roman and Jewish materials, see D. Cartlidge and D. Dungan, *Documents for the Study of the Gospels* (Philadelphia: Fortress Press, 1980). For comparison among the Synoptic Gospels, see B. H. Throckmorton, *Gospel Parallels: A Comparison of the Synoptic Gospels*, 5th ed. (Nashville: Thomas Nelson, 1992). Information on a wide range of questions concerning the Gospels is provided by J. B. Green and S. McKnight (eds.), *Dictionary of Jesus and the Gospels* (Downer's Grove, IL: InterVarsity Press, 1992). L. T. Johnson, *The Writings of the New Testament: An Interpretation*, revised edition with the assistance of Todd Penner (Minneapolis: Fortress Press, 1999), provides a more extensive discussion of background issues, the canonical Gospels, and the development of canonization, as well as an extensive bibliography.

Supplementary Reading:

Allen, C. *The Human Christ: The Search for the Historical Jesus*. New York: The Free Press, 1998. An elegantly written intellectual history that places the quest for Jesus within broader European and American cultural forces.

Allison, D.C., Jr. *The New Moses: A Matthean Typology*. Minneapolis: Fortress Press, 1993. The author of a scholarly commentary on Matthew shows how the evangelist's use of Torah shapes his narration and theology.

Ball, D. M. "'I Am' in John's Gospel: Literary Function, Background, and Theological Implications." *Journal for the Study of New Testament Supplements*, 124; Sheffield: Sheffield Academic Press, 1996. As the lengthy title suggests, this is a scholarly examination of a strain of language in the Fourth Gospel that communicates the divinity of Jesus.

Barrett, C. K. *The Gospel of John and Judaism*. Translated by D. M. Smith. Philadelphia: Fortress Press, 1975. Author of a classic set of essays on John, as well as a critical commentary, Barrett considers the diverse aspects of the Fourth Gospel's relationship to Judaism.

Best, E. *Disciples and Discipleship: Studies in the Gospel According to Mark*. Edinburgh: T & T Clark, 1986. A veteran student of Mark's Gospel devotes a set of studies to his curiously negative portrayal of the church's future leaders.

Boring, M. E. *The Continuing Voice of Jesus: Christian Prophecy and the Gospel Tradition*. Louisville: Westminster/John Knox Press, 1991. A thorough examination of the complex interplay between ecstatic utterances in early Christian worship and the shaping of the memory of Jesus.

Brown, R. E. *The Birth of the Messiah*, enlarged ed. New York: Doubleday, 1993. This highly influential work led a generation of scholars to understand the infancy accounts in Matthew and Luke as forms of Jewish midrash.

————. *The Death of the Messiah: From Gethsemane to the Grave*. 2 vols. New York: Doubleday, 1994. A magisterial treatment of the passion accounts of the canonical Gospels, including historical and literary analysis. The second volume contains a number of appendices, one dealing with the relationship of the Gospel of Peter to the canonical tradition.

————. *The Gospel According to John*. 2 vols. Anchor Bible; New York: Doubleday, 1966–1970. A remarkably full and balanced consideration of the Fourth Gospel that pays close attention to all critical issues and is sensitive to the layered nature of John's narrative.

Bultmann, R. *The History of the Synoptic Tradition*. Translated by J. Marsh. Revised edition. New York: Harper and Row, 1968. An updated edition of the early-20th-century study that basically invented the form of criticism of the New Testament and is still a necessary reference for those working in the field.

————. *The Gospel of John: A Commentary*. Translated by G. R. Beasley-Murray. Philadelphia: Westminster, 1971. The classic commentary on the Fourth Gospel, deeply flawed by its source theories and postulates about Gnostic influence but brilliant in its imaginative grasp of the Gospel's religious sensibility.

Burridge, R. A. *What Are the Gospels? A Comparison with Graeco-Roman Biography*. Societas Novi Testamenti Studiorum Monograph Series 70; Cambridge: Cambridge University Press, 1992. A careful consideration of the gospel genre, taking up the challenge posed by C. H. Talbert that the Gospels are best understood as Hellenistic biographies.

Cadbury, H. J. *The Making of Luke-Acts*. New York: Macmillan Co., 1927. This older work by a great scholar in Luke-Acts is one of the best books on a New Testament Gospel ever written, arguing that the Gospel and Acts should be read together and setting a scholarly agenda for several generations.

Catchpole, D. *The Quest for Q*. Edinburgh: T & T Clark, 1993. A readable and reasonably balanced account of scholarship devoted to the putative source used independently by Matthew and Luke in the composition of their Gospels.

Cohen, S. J. D. *From the Maccabees to the Mishnah*. Philadelphia: Westminster Press, 1987. A well-informed and readable survey of historical movements and ideological developments in Palestinian Judaism before and after the rise of Christianity.

Crossan, J. D. *The Cross That Spoke: The Origins of the Passion Narrative*. San Francisco: Harper and Row, 1988. The prolific and provocative leader of the Jesus Seminar argues that the Gospel of Peter represents an independent witness to the resurrection and to the process by which the evangelists constructed history out of prophecy.

————. *The Historical Jesus: The Life of a Mediterranean Jewish Peasant*. San Francisco: HarperCollins, 1991. One of the most thorough, methodologically consistent, and interesting of the contemporary efforts to construct a usable Jesus; Crossan is candid about his techniques and purposes.

Dahl, N. A. "The Purpose of Mark's Gospel," in *Jesus in the Memory of the Church*, pp. 52–65. Minneapolis: Augsburg Press, 1976. One of the great New Testament scholars of the 20th century shows how Mark's narrative is shaped as a teaching on discipleship to the evangelist's community.

Dibelius, M. *From Tradition to Gospel*. Translated by R. Woolf. New York: Charles Scribner's Sons, 1934. With R. Bultmann, one of the founders of New Testament form criticism, Dibelius emphasized the social contexts within which the memory of Jesus was selected and shaped by oral tradition.

Donahue, J. R. *Are You the Christ? The Trial Narrative in the Gospel of Mark*. Society of Biblical Literature Dissertation Series 10; Missoula: Scholars Press, 1973. An early and fruitful application of redaction criticism to Mark's passion account, showing the purposefulness of its shaping.

Ferguson, E. *Backgrounds of Early Christianity*, 2nd ed. Grand Rapids: Eerdmans, 1993. A well-informed and responsible survey of the various cultural forces at work in the period immediately before and after the rise of Christianity.

Foskett, M. F. *A Virgin Conceived: Mary and Classical Representations of Virginity*. Bloomington: Indiana University Press, 2002. A fine example of the fruitfulness of comparative analysis, this study shows how the theme of virginity works quite differently in the Gospel of Luke and the *Protevangelium Jacobi*.

Garrett, S. *The Demise of the Devil: Magic and the Demonic in Luke's Writings*. Minneapolis: Fortress Press, 1989. An original and insightful study of Luke's construal of Jesus's proclamation of the kingdom of God and how that proclamation demanded battle against the spiritual powers that oppress humans.

Grant, R. *Gnosticism and Early Christianity*, rev. ed. New York: Harper and Row, 1966. An argument that stresses the Jewish origins of Gnosticism, finding its roots in disappointed apocalyptic expectations.

Harnack, A. *History of Dogma*, vol. 1. Translated by N. Buchanan. Theological Translation Library; London: Williams and Norgate, 1905. This is the classic statement concerning the origins of Gnosticism as the "acute Hellenization of Christianity," based on the available texts before Nag Hammadi.

Hock, R. F. *The Life of Mary and Birth of Jesus: The Ancient Infancy Gospel of James*. Edited by R. Riegert. Berkeley, CA: Ulysses Press, 1997. A translation and study of the *Protevangelium Jacobi* by an eminent authority.

———. *The Infancy Gospels of James and Thomas*. Santa Rosa, CA: Polebridge Press, 1995. A leading authority provides introduction, notes, and the original Greek texts, as well as translations of the two earliest and most influential infancy gospels.

Johnson, L. T. *The Gospel of Luke* and *The Acts of the Apostles*. Sacra Pagina. Collegeville, MN: The Liturgical Press, 1991 and 1992. These commentaries follow the narrative development of Luke's two-volume work closely and provide the exegetical basis for the lectures on this Gospel.

———. *The Literary Function of Possessions in Luke-Acts*. Society of Biblical Literature Dissertation Series 39. Missoula: Scholars Press, 1977. A literary study that shows how Luke's extraordinary attention to the disposition of material possessions by the characters in his narrative serves a larger purpose in the story of the prophet and the people.

———. *Living Jesus: Learning the Heart of the Gospel*. San Francisco: HarperSanFrancisco, 1999. An accessible examination of the multiple ways in which the conviction that Jesus is resurrected leads to diverse ways of learning him, with special attention to the ways in which Jesus is interpreted in the Gospels and other New Testament writings.

―――――. *The Real Jesus: The Misguided Quest for the Historical Jesus and the Truth of the Traditional Gospels*. San Francisco: HarperSanFrancisco, 1996. A critical assessment of historical Jesus studies since 1990, with particular and negative attention to the theological agenda at work in the Jesus Seminar and similar ventures.

Jonas, H. *The Gnostic Religion: The Message of the Alien God and the Beginnings of Christianity*, 2nd ed. Boston: Beacon Press, 1963. Jonas argues that a pessimistic and dualistic tendency was at work throughout the early Roman Empire because of the experience of social alienation; a powerful but overly simple explanation.

Kermode, F. *The Genesis of Secrecy: On the Interpretation of Narrative*. Cambridge: Harvard University Press, 1979. A brilliant and influential study of Mark's narrative techniques by a British literary critic, who uncovers the layers of irony in Mark's composition.

Kloppenborg, J. S. *The Formation of Q: Trajectories in Ancient Wisdom Collections*. Philadelphia: Fortress Press, 1987. A leading scholar in Q research lays out the argument for regarding the material shared by Matthew and Luke—but not found in Mark—as a distinct and coherent composition, indeed one in which distinct stages of development can be discerned.

Layton, B., ed. *The Rediscovery of Gnosticism: Proceedings of the International Conference on Gnosticism at Yale, New Haven, Connecticut, March 28–31, 1978*. 2 vols. Studies in the History of Religions 41; Leiden: Brill, 1980–1981. A collection of studies that advances the position concerning the Nag Hammadi library that two distinct forms of Gnosticism (Valentinian and Sethian) are found therein.

Logan, A. H. B. *Gnostic Truth and Christian Heresy: A Study in the History of Gnosticism*. Peabody, MA: Hendrickson Publishers, 1996. An extensive argument concerning the relationship of "Sethian" Gnosticism to Christianity through the placement of the *Apocryphon of John* as the central mythic text of Gnosticism.

Luedemann, G. "The Successors of Pre-70 Jerusalem Christianity: A Critical Evaluation of the Pella Tradition," in *Jewish and Christian Self-Definition*, pp. 1:161–173. Edited by E. P. Sanders. Philadelphia: Fortress Press, 1980. A thorough attempt to test the historicity of the legendary accounts of the Ebionites and other Jewish Christian groups.

Martyn, J. L. *History and Theology in the Fourth Gospel*, rev. ed. Nashville: Abingdon Press, 1979. An extremely influential study of John that argues for the historical setting of separation from the synagogue as the factor that shapes the symbolism of the narrative.

Matera, F. J. *The Kingship of Jesus: Composition and Theology in Mark 15*. Society of Biblical Literature Dissertation Series 66; Chico: Scholars Press, 1982. A careful analysis of the death of Jesus in Mark that touches on the specific theological interests of the evangelist reflected in the account.

McDonald, L. M. *The Formation of the Christian Bible Canon*, rev. ed. Peabody, MA: Hendrickson Publishers, 1995. A thorough and responsible examination of the process of canonization in Christianity, cognizant of the most recent scholarship on the issue.

McKnight, E. *What Is Form Criticism?* Guides to Biblical Study; Philadelphia: Fortress Press, 1969. An accessible and responsible treatment of the discipline that seeks to find units of oral tradition in written compositions, with examples.

Meeks, W. A. "Am I a Jew? Johannine Christianity and Judaism," in *Christianity, Judaism and other Greco-Roman Cults*, pp. 163–186. Edited by J. Neusner. Studies in Judaism in Late Antiquity 12; Leiden: Brill, 1975. One of the leading scholars on the Fourth Gospel takes up the complex issue of John's relationship to contemporary Judaism.

———. "The Man from Heaven in Johannine Sectarianism," *Journal of Biblical Literature* 91 (1972): 44–72. An essay that has shaped all subsequent study of John, arguing that the literary technique of irony used by the author of John serves to accentuate the distance between insider and outsider.

Meier, J. P. *A Marginal Jew: Rethinking the Historical Jesus*. 3 vols. New York: Doubleday, 1991, 1994. Perhaps the most ambitious effort at reconstructing the historical Jesus ever undertaken; still unfinished, these three volumes are marked by careful analysis and compendious scholarship.

————. *Law and History in Matthew's Gospel: A Redactional Study of 5:17–48*. Rome: Biblical Institute Press, 1976. Before Meier turned to historical Jesus research, he was a leading scholar on Matthew; this study takes on the heart of the Sermon on the Mount, showing its distinctive Matthean traits.

————. *The Vision of Matthew: Christ, Church, and Morality in the First Gospel*. New York: Crossroad, 1991. The author shows how the three dimensions (understanding of Jesus, moral instruction, and the shaping of the church) intertwine in Matthew's carefully crafted Gospel.

Moessner, D. *Lord of the Banquet: The Literary and Theological Significance of the Lukan Travel Narrative*. Minneapolis: Fortress Press, 1989. An ambitious effort to show that the construction of the travel account in Luke 9–19 imitates Deuteronomy and presents Jesus as "the prophet like Moses."

Moule, C. F. D. *The Birth of the New Testament*, 3rd ed. New York: Harper and Row, 1982. A clearly written and successful attempt to locate the development of traditions within living communities of faith and to show how the New Testament is "birthed" by this process.

Munck, J. "Jewish Christianity in Post-Apostolic Times," *New Testament Studies* 6 (1959–60): 103–116. A survey and assessment of the known evidence concerning the various groups claiming an allegiance to Judaism within the Christian movement.

Neyrey, J. H. *The Passion According to Luke: A Redaction Study of Luke's Soteriology*. New York: Paulist Press, 1985. A set of carefully observed and well-argued exegetical essays on various aspects of Luke's passion account.

O'Day, G. *Revelation in the Fourth Gospel: Narrative Mode and Theological Claim*. Philadelphia: Fortress Press, 1986. An exceptionally close reading of the narrative texture of John's Gospel and how the shaping of that narrative advances the religious purposes of the composition.

Overmann, A. *Matthew's Gospel and Formative Judaism: The Social World of the Matthean Community*. Minneapolis: Fortress Press, 1990. A convincing display of the evidence that supports the notion of Matthew's Gospel being composed with an eye to the "synagogue down the street."

Pagels, E. *The Gnostic Gospels*. New York: Vintage Books, 1981. Less a study of Gnosticism than an argument in favor of Gnostic sensibilities, this bestselling book has had a major impact on those challenging the traditional canon of the New Testament.

Patterson, S. J. *The Gospel of Thomas and Jesus*. Sonoma: Polebridge Press, 1993. A good representative of the position that the Coptic Gospel found at Nag Hammadi contains sayings as old as those found in the canonical Gospels and, therefore, is a primary source for reconstructing the teaching of Jesus.

Pelikan, J. *Jesus through the Centuries: His Place in the History of Culture*. New York: Perennial Library, 1987. The greatest contemporary historian of Christianity traces the continuing life of Jesus through literature, theology, and art.

Perrin, N. *What Is Redaction Criticism?* Guides to Biblical Study; Philadelphia: Fortress Press, 1969. A leading proponent of this method of studying the Gospels demonstrates its usefulness when applied to the section of Mark following the confession of Peter.

Robbins, V. K. *Jesus the Teacher: A Socio-Rhetorical Interpretation of Mark*. Philadelphia: Fortress Press, 1984. A comparative study of Mark that takes seriously the context of the social and literary environment, especially on the Greco-Roman side.

Rudolph, K. *Gnosis: The Nature and History of Gnosticism*. Translated by R. M. Wilson. San Francisco: Harper and Row, 1983. A synthetic study of this complex religious phenomenon by an acknowledged master in the field.

Saldarini, A. J. *Matthew's Christian-Jewish Community*. Chicago: University of Chicago Press, 1994. Written by a scholar exceptionally well-versed in Pharisaic traditions, this study shows the complexity of Matthew's engagement with formative Judaism.

Schweitzer, A. *The Quest of the Historical Jesus*. Translated by W. Montgomery. Baltimore: Johns Hopkins Press, 1998. This is a reprint of the classic 1906 study that interpreted—and, in some respects, invented—the first "quest" in critical scholarship (especially German scholarship).

Segovia, F. F. *The Farewell of the Word: The Johannine Call to Abide*. Minneapolis: Fortress Press, 1991. A literary-redactional study of the farewell discourse of the Fourth Gospel that develops the distinctive Johannine understanding of the relationship among God, Jesus, and the disciples.

Stein, R. H. *The Synoptic Problem: An Introduction*. Grand Rapids: Baker Books, 1987. A clear and balanced presentation of the data, the critical questions, and the major solutions offered with regard to the tangled literary relationship among Matthew, Mark, and Luke.

Stendahl, K. *The School of St. Matthew and Its Use of the Old Testament*. Philadelphia: Fortress Press, 1968. A pioneering work on Matthew's distinctive way of engaging Torah, arguing that its careful engagement with scripture took place in a school context.

Talbert, C. H. *What Is a Gospel? The Genre of the Canonical Gospels*. Philadelphia: Fortress Press, 1977. A serious effort to place the Gospels in the context of Greco-Roman biographies, arguing on analogy with the biographies of philosophers that the Gospels serve to correct readers' views through the construction of the "life and teachings of Jesus."

Tannehill, R. C. *The Narrative Unity of Luke-Acts: A Literary Interpretation*. 2 vols. Philadelphia: Fortress Press, 1986, 1990. A major effort to interpret the two Lukan volumes as a single literary work, notable for the careful attention to narrative development of themes.

Telford, W. R., ed. *The Interpretation of Mark*. Issues in Religion and Theology 7; Edinburgh: T & T Clark, 1995. A collection of classic essays in the history of the critical interpretation of Mark's Gospel.

Tiede, D. L. *Prophecy and History in Luke-Acts*. Philadelphia: Fortress Press, 1980. A strong argument for the theological shaping of Luke's historical narrative along the lines of the fulfillment of prophecy, as well as the acceptance and rejection of God's prophet.

Tuckett, C. M. *Nag Hammadi and the Gospel Tradition*. Edited by John Riches. Edinburgh: T & T Clark, 1986. A careful examination of the claims made for the originality of the Jesus traditions in the Nag

Hammadi texts, concluding that there is a strong probability for dependence on the canonical Gospels.

Turner, M. L. *The Gospel According to Philip: The Sources and Coherence of an Early Christian Collection*. Leiden: Brill, 1996. A scholarly study of the apparent literary incoherence of the Gnostic composition and an effort to make sense of its many dimensions.

Von Voorst, R. E. *The Ascents of James: History and Theology of a Jewish Christian Community*. Society of Biblical Literature Dissertation Series 112; Atlanta: Scholars Press, 1989. A thorough investigation of the literary structure and ideological posture of a portion of the pseudo-Clementine literature that expresses hostility toward Pauline Christianity.

Williams, J. A. *Biblical Interpretation of the Gospel of Truth from Nag Hammadi*. Society of Biblical Literature Dissertation Series 79; Atlanta: Scholars Press, 1988. Undertakes the difficult task of disentangling the strands of biblical echo and allusion in the masterpiece of Valentinian Gnosticism.

Williams, M. A. *Rethinking "Gnosticism": An Argument for Dismantling a Dubious Category*. Princeton: Princeton University Press, 1996. A bold and well-argued call to return to the beginning in the study of the ancient texts usually associated with Gnosticism.

Wilson, R. M. *The Gospel of Philip: Translated from the Coptic Text with Introduction and Commentary*. New York: Harper and Row, 1962. Wilson is one of the pioneering figures in British scholarship, devoted to Gnosticism and known for his careful analysis and judicious conclusions.